DATE DUE

NOV 2 3 1994	JUN 2 7 2002	
JAN 1 2 1995	JAN 0 2 2003	
NOV 9 1995	AUG 2 5 2004	
DEC 0 7 1995	NOV 1 6 2004	
FEB 1 0 1996	FEB 1 8 2005	
MAR 2 7 1997		
DEC 2 1997		
MAR 1 1 2000		
JUL - 6 2000		
NOV 1 6 2000		
DEC 1 5 2000		
MAR 2 2002		

IAN
TYSON

IAN TYSON

I NEVER SOLD MY SADDLE

with
Colin Escott

GREYSTONE BOOKS
Douglas & McIntyre
Vancouver/Toronto

94 95 96 97 98   5 4 3 2 1

Greystone Books
A division of Douglas & McIntyre Ltd.
1615 Venables Street
Vancouver, British Columbia V5L 2H1

Canadian Cataloguing in Publication Data
Tyson, Ian, 1933-
    Ian Tyson

    "Greystone Books."
    ISBN 1-55054-178-1
1. Tyson, Ian, 1933-   2. Country musicians—Canada—Biography.
I. Escott, Colin.   II. Title.
ML420.T97A3 1994   782.421642'092   C94-910462-0

A Peregrine Smith Book, published simultaneously in the United States by
Gibbs Smith, Publisher
P.O. Box 667
Layton, Utah 84041

Design by Mary Ellen Thompson
Cover photograph by Ellen Brodylo and Mike Morrow
Scenic illustrations used throughout the book © Rygh Westby
Saddle illustration on front cover and title page by Thomas J. Sanker, © 1993
    Gibbs Smith, Publisher
Printed and bound in Canada by D. W. Friesen & Sons Ltd.

Contents

Ian and Thom Moon at the 1989 Edmonton Folk Festival. Photograph © by Peter Sutherland.

The Ian Tyson Band on the cover of *Old Corrals and Sagebrush* album, 1982. From left to right—Nathan Tinkham, Ian, Thom Moon, Danny McBride, Melvin Wilson, Richard Harrow (standing), and David Wilkie. Photograph © by Jay Dusard.

Introduction

I started them fillies at the pens this mornin'
You know the buckskin and the bay.
Before the wind started blowin' too hard
At the mid part of the day
The driest spring in ninety-one years
The radio played on.
Irving Berlin is a hundred years old today
The wind's gone and blown my woman away.
—("Irving Berlin Is 100 Years
Old Today," Ian Tyson)

Ian Tyson is sixty years old today. It was raining earlier, but now the clouds are rising like a petticoat up the Rockies. The coulees on the eastern face are full of snow. They look like cotton bolls from Ian's porch. Friends are up from Nevada and Wyoming. Ian's wife, Twylla, has just arrived home. The driveway is full. The T-Bar-Y ranch is slowly winding down for the day. The cutting pens are empty, and so is the Suzy Bogguss Arena, the indoor training arena Ian constructed with the proceeds from Suzy's recording of his song "Someday Soon." Everyone is looking forward to being in rough shape tomorrow.

Jonesy and Blaine are out on the porch. Jonesy is singing a song. A cowboy song, of course. Ian is in an expansive mood. It's been two weeks since he gave up chewing tobacco, he tells everyone. It's as tough as giving up smoking. He allows that chewing's okay as long as you do it occasionally, but he was going through a lid every two days. Ian's telling stories, doing impersonations, making politically incorrect remarks. Creeping socialism, reliance upon the state, school buses pulling up at even the most remote door. The individual has lost his sense of self-reliance and self-worth. There's a shortage of damned ol' cowboy pride in the world. Country music for sure isn't what it used to be either. Garth Brooks. Looks like a little feedlot guy with a cane. Ian doesn't get it. But if Garth's so damn keen on putting cowboy songs on his albums, Ian's got one or two he could flog him.

Out here, near High River, Alberta, all the songs, and all the images in Ian Tyson's music start to acquire a sense of place. The bald eagles staring you down unfazed and unfrightened, the coyotes yowling into the night. The Rockies just half an hour to the west, always changing color. The big sky. The wind always blowing; sometimes in winter it gets teeth that'll tear the door off your pickup just when you thought the worst of your day was over and you'd made it home.

Ian Tyson is a cowboy, pridefully a working cowboy, but he can stand back and consider what he does with the dispassion of an outsider and the soul of a poet. He's a part of the cowboy culture, yet he can put that necessary bit of distance between himself and his subject and capture images that are too close to the workaday reality of the cowboy's life for him to think twice about them. Perhaps Tyson can put that necessary distance between him and his subject because he has lived other lives.

The cowboy is the most enduring image in North American culture. Just when he appears to have ridden off into the sunset for good, he returns. He represents the nexus between land, beast, and man that was the nexus by which man survived on this earth for three millennia or more and one that is now on the verge of agronomic extinction. More than that, the cowboy stands for self-reliance in an era when the state mollycoddles us from birth to senility. The cowboy holds out hope for personal reinvention in a new land, a potential now all but unrealizable because the bloom is fading on the new land. It has been mapped, criss-crossed with roads, marked, measured, pocked with subdivisions, and dotted with satellite dishes. A Wal-Mart is coming soon, and the campfire is going out.

The global village is a reality. The telephone and the fax machine bring the world to Ian Tyson's door. Fed-Ex may not deliver out here yet, but some damn fool gave out directions to the Tyson ranch, so tourists reckon they can drive up his driveway with the Betacam rolling. As he looks around him, Ian can't find many grounds for optimism, long-term optimism that is, about the land he loves. Personally, he's secure and has a good life, but much of what he holds dear is on the verge of extinction. What of it will be left for his daughter, Adelita Rose? Oh, to have stood a hundred years ago where he stands now, looking out over a vast, unfenced, untreed prairie to the east and to the pre-national-parked Rockies to the west.

Ian Tyson's personal future is secure because, as a singer, he beat the odds and got two kicks at the can. Most entertainers count themselves lucky to have one. For a decade or so, he was half of Ian & Sylvia. They didn't sell as many records as Bob Dylan or Peter Paul & Mary, but no one who so much as flitted through the folk counter-culture of the sixties can fail to remember Ian's songs "Four Strong Winds" and "Someday Soon," or Sylvia's "You Were On My Mind." Those songs formed part of the collective unconscious of the sixties. They've been deleted, left for dead, reissued, Muzaked, and still every few years someone records one of them. As songs, they keep passing this way again—and likely always will.

Then, in the eighties, after taking his own advice and heading out to Alberta, Ian began making new western music. Forty years ago, an editor at a music trade paper in New York conjoined country and western in a marriage of convenience, and the two have been confused ever since. But Ian writes western music, not country music. His is the first new western music since the era of the television themes back in the late fifties and early sixties, and the first authentic new western music in several generations. One of his albums, *Cowboyography*, went gold in Canada, and is closing in on platinum. Astonishing for a song cycle that can only truly be understood by no more than a few thousand people in the whole of North America. If nothing else, it shows how important the cowboy still is to us and how many still want to identify with him, even those who don't know which end of a horse gets up first.

Ian Tyson's cowboy image is no affectation. He is no weekend cowboy with an apartment in town. He'll be opening the barn door in the teeth of a blizzard this winter and following the ups and downs of the cattle market with more than passing interest. He was born to wear a high-crowned hat and a bandanna. He has the horseman's gait—stiff from too many falls, from the pins in his ankle, aggravated now by a touch of arthritis. He has the old cowboy's gift for telling tales with arcane detail and dry humor. Few can spin out a story like that anymore. Even truckers, after hours alone in their cabs, seem to keep it short and to-the-point. Everyone's

"If he wants to be cuttin' a couple of years from now,
Ah, but there's magic in the horses' feet,
In the way they jump and the way they sweep.
It's an addiction—not that hard to understand."
—*("Non Pro Song," Ian Tyson)*

always running late. Expatiation, just telling a long-winded story for the sake of telling it, because there's no phone to answer, no television to watch, is another dying art.

The Ian Tyson story is one of loss and personal redemption; it's of trying to interpret what the little voice within is saying and being true to it. In broader terms, it's about cowboy pride, minority pride, and about keeping a vestige of the old west and its culture safe from the neutering tendencies of mass culture. It's also a story about an obsession that would not be denied, and an affirmation that our basic character is formed early and that we're happiest when we're in touch with it.

George Tyson, Alberta, Canada, 1907.

Ian, age three.

The Leaving of Liverpool

Child apart from the children
Child of make-believe mornings . . .
It's your life, do with your life
Just what you were born to,
Always look up—never look down.
                    —("Child Apart," Ian Tyson)

George Dawson Tyson left Liverpool, England in 1906 bound for the Dominion of Canada. He died in 1968, the year after the hundredth anniversary of Canadian confederation. He arrived on the Prairies not long after the buffalo had gone and just before the range was fenced in, and he lived almost long enough to see buffalo burgers at some of the tonier spots in his adopted hometown of Victoria, British Columbia. He followed a pattern set by British expatriates elsewhere; he escaped the claustrophobic little island, but once he had settled abroad he overemphasized his Britishness and lived as part of an expat colony locked in a curious time warp. Ian likes to call his father "the remittance man," in lore the ne'er do well living out of the country on money sent from home. Whether that is a true characterization or not, the Tyson family was well-off in England, and George Dawson Tyson always knew that at some point he would inherit.

"We went to England in 1951. I think my dad was sniffing around for the inheritance. The old man, my grandfather, was wonderful. Edward Dawson Tyson. A stately old man. He lived with two maiden daughters, Nellie and Dolly. I was sixteen or seventeen. Raging hormones. It was lost on me. We were there a week, and it was like an eternity.

"My dad told me a lot of stuff, but he was a selective raconteur. Edward Tyson was a man of means, and he lived to be an old, old man. He didn't die until my father was in his late sixties. Then the big inheritance that everyone had been waiting for came down, but it wasn't that big when it finally happened. The English government got it all, I guess. My dad and my mom got a trip to the old country. By the time my dad died, he was seventy-nine and there wasn't much left."

After he arrived in Canada, George Tyson went to the Bowden-Innisfail area north of Calgary, and worked as a ranch hand. He stayed about three years, making it as a cowboy, then drifting out to the west coast around 1910. He homesteaded on Vancouver Island for a while, its climate so much like the land he had left behind, then went off to fight for the old country in the Great War.

Ian, age eleven.

"They were cannon fodder for the British Army. He was damn near the only one who got back. His father bought him a commission in the British Army. He became an instant captain. Saved his life. He won a Military Cross. 'MC and Bar, boy,' he'd say. They had the cenotaph built by the time he got out of hospital and back to Vancouver Island, and his name was about the only one that wasn't on the damn thing. He went back to Duncan, which is a yuppie playground now, but was Eden then. He went from Eden, to hell, to Purgatory, and back. Most of those old buggers, their British accents would get stronger as they got older. They were crazy old guys. A lot of them had been gassed, I guess."

George Tyson buried his dreams of becoming a rancher along with his buddies. He married Margaret Campbell and started selling insurance. She was Scottish Presbyterian. Ian once said she equated fun with sin. In 1873, her father had left Petrolia, Ontario and opened the first drugstore on Canada's west coast. Shortly after George and Margaret married, George returned to Alberta for a few years selling real estate during the oil boom. His family stayed back on Vancouver Island. No one ever spoke much about that period. There were two children; a daughter, Jean, born on April 12, 1931, and a son, Ian Dawson Tyson, born in Victoria Hospital on September 25, 1933. Money from Margaret's inheritance paid for Ian to go to private school on Vancouver Island.

That Ian would one day be a rancher would have been just about conceivable, perhaps even laudable, to George Tyson, once a man of similar dreams. Ian Dawson Tyson—gentleman rancher would have had the right ring to it. But that Ian would embrace the cowboy life and sing about cowboys would have been broaching the unthinkable.

"Cowboys were trash. Glorifying the life in song was out of the question. The old man would put them down. 'Oh cowboys . . . never a dollar to their name . . . Sell insurance, boy. Good. Reliable.' He'd huff and he'd puff. He never figured on the romance of the cowboy and the leisure industry. He never figured out the myth. Buffalo Bill did—but my old man didn't.

"Old George wasn't a horseman. He loved horses, but when it came to horses he didn't know shit from apple butter. He'd just jump on and go. He didn't know what made them tick, what made them stop, what made them turn around. He was the same way when he went fishing. He never figured anything out. He certainly never figured out the insurance business.

"The first cowboy I ever saw was when the rodeo came to town and my dad took me. I was maybe four or five. I saw this Indian. He was dark as mahogany, and he had a purple silk shirt. He lifted me up and stuck me on the saddle. I said, 'That's it.'"

Contradictorily, as George Tyson poohpoohed the cowboys, he was feeding his son's imagination with Will James books. Will James's life was a lie, a wonderful lie, and one more fascinating than any tale he ever told. It was a lie that ended up killing him. "Will James" was a French Canadian, Joseph Dufault, born in 1892 in what is now called St. Nazaire d'Acton in Quebec's eastern townships. In 1907 he headed west, talking about becoming a cowboy. By all accounts, he did it, but in 1915 he found himself in jail in Nevada for rustling. After he was released, he began writing and drawing. His drawings were lithe and vivid evocations of cowboy life with an almost palpable sense of movement. His books sold in the millions, and his horse, Smoky, was almost as popular and as well known for a while as Black Beauty.

Ian, age twelve with his favorite pony, Steel.

In 1930, Will James wrote what was supposed to be his autobiography. It was called *Lone Cowboy—My Life Story*, and it was an almost complete fabrication. Accounting for his accent, he said that his father, supposedly a Texan, had been fatally gored by a steer and he had been brought up by "Bopy" Beaupre, a French-Canadian trapper. Will James lived in fear that someone would unmask him. He erected a wall of lies around him, then couldn't escape from it. He started drinking heavily. The drinking killed him.

"Dick Farnsworth is a good friend of mine, and he met Will James. He's the only person I knew who met him. They were testing horses for a James movie of *Smoky*. He said James was so drunk he'd pissed on himself. I said, 'Dick, I've gotta know, did Will James have this French-Canadian accent?' I'd heard he'd never been able to shake it, and he'd invented this story to account for his accent, but Dick said, 'Naw, he sounded like a New Mexico cowboy.'"

Ian was one of millions of boys transfixed by the twenty-four books, like *Smoky the Cowhorse*, that James wrote. Will James inspired Ian to draw. Even Ian's handwriting and hand-lettering have some of the character of Will James.

"Will James died in 1942. His liver collapsed. The last few months are cloudy because he was in North Hollywood in a bungalow, and there's this mysterious Jewish woman who nobody knows who's in photographs with him. His wife, Alice, had been gone for years. He drove her over the brink. His ranch was gone, but he had this little house in Billings, Montana. It's still there."

Will James did what people had been doing for a generation and continue to do to this day. He reinvented himself in the west and brought to his new life the zeal of the fresh convert. There, in the vastness and newness, a man could truly believe he'd left everything behind. George Tyson tried it to a lesser extent; Will James to an almost absurd extent.

Bob Nolan, another whose life offers some parallels to Ian's, fits the same mold. Originally from the Canadian province of New Brunswick, he moved to Tucson then on to Los Angeles. There, he answered an advertisement for a harmony singer that had been placed by Leonard Slye, an Ohioan who was about to shed his old skin and become Roy Rogers. Later, Rogers and Nolan would form the core of the Sons of the Pioneers, the most popular western singing group of all time. Nolan wrote the Pioneers' most memorable songs, "Way Out There," "Cool Water," "Tumbling Tumbleweeds," "Wind," "Chant of the Wanderer." They were songs that couldn't have been written by someone who had lived all his life in the west because their magic lay in the outsider's sense of wonder. Nolan's songs were the last great western songs before Ian Tyson redrew the rules of western song craft fifty years later.

"I reinvented myself in the west. Jay Dusard, the cowboy photographer, always said, 'Tyson was born west of the west. He had to go east.' It's true. Like the song says, I used to ask myself, 'What would Will

Will James

When I was but a small boy,
My father bought me many books
'bout the creatures of the riverbanks
And the sins of old sea cooks.
But the ones I never left behind
With the old forgotten games
Were the tales of wild and windy slopes
By the man they call Will James.

Ah, the living of his cowboy dreams
Or so it seemed to me.
The perfect combination
Of riding high and living free.
His heroes were his horses
And he drew them clear and true,
On every page they'd come alive
And jump straight out at you.

His race toward the sunset
Was the high and lonesome kind.
Like a coyote always looking back
He left no tracks behind.
So I've memorized those pictures, boys
They're still the very best.
If whiskey was his mistress,
His true love was the west.

I remember up on Dead Man's Creek
Back thirty years and more
I hired on to breaking colts,
Which I'd never done before.
A city kid, I asked myself,
Now what would Will James do?
And you know it was the damndest thing
But it kinda got me through.

—(Ian Tyson)

Ian, age thirteen.

James do?' It really was the damndest thing. I did the whole thing right out of a book, and I got away with it because I was young and tough and the horses weren't too rank. I was an instant cowboy, courtesy of Will James."

The first stop was a blind alley. It was the Vancouver School of Art, then in the grip of post-impressionism. The local hero was Emily Carr, who painted the rain forest and Indian carvings. One couldn't, as Ian says, get away with a brush stroke in oils less than half an inch wide. The city of Vancouver still had some of its original character; it had, after all, been home to the first Skid Row and had grown up to serve the logging industry. The old wooden fire-traps were still there, and Ian had his studio on the fourth floor of one, three or four blocks from school.

"We were all broke, stealing jars of peanut butter. Marking time, I guess. I shared studio space with Nancy Patterson,

Glenlyon School soccer team, 1946–1947. Ian is the first seated boy on the right. Photograph by Robert Park.

Ian, age seventeen, with Mt. Assiniboine wrangling crew and cooks.

who won every scholarship as we went along and deservedly so. The rest of us were scrambling, but she had her style figured out. She was hanging out with Gordie Cox, a disbarred jockey and would-be jazz drummer from the States, and he and I were buddies. Gordie had the first edition ever seen in Vancouver of *On the Road*, by Jack Kerouac, which left a strong impression on all of us, myself especially.

"I never really liked the cubists, abstract impressionists, and post-impressionists we studied. I wanted to be able to do the fine detail, but it was very much frowned upon, as was the realistic or photographic mode. You wouldn't do the silver concho on the bridle that the great western painters did. Consequently, I never learned small detail with oils. People who went south to work for Disney were frowned upon as well; there was no appreciation of literal art, cartoon art, or illustrative art. If I'd had the focus to do good literal art, they might have gone along with it, but I was just giving in to peer pressure."

Equally, the music of the late forties and early fifties left little lasting impression on Ian. Strangely so, because most musicians know that they are going to be musicians from the time they first remember and soak up any music, all music. Just as art school left Ian with little that he carried forward, so music was always something in the background. He didn't pick up a guitar or try to sing until he was in his twenties, and it took him a lot longer to find his true voice, longer still to wed his life to his music.

"When I first started singing, I wanted to be a tenor. I wanted to sing that high lonesome style, like Roy Acuff. I'm not a tenor, but it took me years to recognize that. Marty Robbins was a big influence later. Elvis too. At home, when we were growing up, it was what you'd expect, the pop singers of the early fifties—Patti Page, Joni James, Frankie Laine. The only country and western music you could get was Lefty Frizzell and Hank Thompson.

"I started playing guitar in hospital in Calgary around 1956. The guitar was better suited to a guy with no patience than painting. Johnny Cash had 'I Walk The Line' out. That was the first one I tried to play. The kid in the next bed had a guitar. It was still fairly unique then. Not everyone played. We were in the broken-leg ward, and there were about six or seven of us in there. I broke my leg in a little rodeo in Cremona. It's the ankle I still have trouble with. They put pins in, which was unusual then, and the ankle's pretty messed up now.

Ian in 1959, learning to play the guitar.

"I played some country dances out in Port Alberni, plunking away at three chords. It was heavy Ukrainian and Polish out there. You had to play waltzes and schottisches. Every country band had an accordion. I loved it. It was a whole different culture. My running partner, John 'Bugs' Bigelow, played piano, and he was more into the great jazz stuff of that era—like Benny Goodman. I was drifting toward country music even then, and I was playing with a guy called Steve Cresta who was in art school with me. He got me my first gigs with Taller O'Shea and his Pistol Packin' Rhythm."

Then came Elvis. Almost everything that has been said about the cultural impact of Elvis Presley is true. There is simply no telling how many teens wanted to be Elvis. The guitar became omnipresent thanks to Elvis. The music of the black and white underclasses got on prime-time television thanks to Elvis. Ian, who was two and a half years older than Elvis, responded as so many others did to the blind butt-shaking energy of rock 'n' roll. It was so different in that respect from any white popular music up to that point.

"I was in art school, and nothing was happening. I was playing guitar in a rockabilly band, the Sensational Stripes. This guy, Tony Romaise, was an early Chuck Berry-styled guitar player, and they were few on the ground in those days. He took me under his wing. I was trying to sing a little rockabilly, and we were starving. We did Elvis and Buddy Holly. I played a date with Buddy Holly, Eddie Cochran, LaVern Baker, and Paul Anka in 1957. It was a package show, and Union regulations stipulated that they had to have a local added attraction. I heard those Fender amps that Buddy Holly had. They were buzzing and clicking. That was the loudest music I'd ever heard in my life. It just blew me away."

Ian came of age during a golden era. Canada had helped win the War. Its resource-based economy was booming, and the boom appeared certain to stretch indefinitely into the future. Racial and linguistic tensions were barely on simmer. The quiet buoyant optimism was contagious.

"There was always a job. You could go fifteen miles down the road and there was another job. It might not pay a whole lot, but the jobs were always there.

"I had a girlfriend in Los Angeles, a line-bred, British Columbia Greek girl. That was a big affair. She was a very dramatic young girl. Her father was a Greek immigrant. He had landed in New York with a buck in his pocket and had ended up in Vernon, British Columbia in the Okanagan Valley. He opened a restaurant, a hotel, ran the hockey team. She was a strikingly beautiful woman. Dark, gorgeous, and wilder than I was. She came to art school when I was in my third year. She was a freshman and blew everyone away. She had the instructors panting at her feet, but she took a fancy to me. I blew my whole year. We were sneaking off, and it got complicated. Very complicated.

"She had access to economic freedom and went to Los Angeles. She told her parents she was going to a design school there. I drove down to see her once in an old Dodge that died on Grapevine Hill, heading out of Bakersfield. The first person to offer me a ride was Sam Peckinpah. I was wearing a straw hat, looked like a cowboy, and he picked me up. He was doing 'Gunsmoke.' He said, 'If you're starving, come on out. Can you ride?' I said, 'Shit, I can ride anything.' He gave me his card, but I didn't see him again for twenty-five years, not until he was directing *Pat Garrett and Billy the Kid* with Kris Kristofferson. I never took him up on his offer at the time. My girlfriend ran me off. I hitchhiked back home."

Ian graduated from the Vancouver School of Art in 1958. He'd ridden in a few rodeos, learned basic chords on the guitar, hammered out three-chord rockabilly, learned commercial art and design, but none of those could keep him around Vancouver. The call to the road came from Jack Kerouac, the one writer to have as profound an influence on Ian as Will James. *On The Road* was both beacon and bible to the first post-nuclear generation. The book was populated by what Kerouac himself liked to call "angelheaded hipsters" who took to the highways, the freights, and the jazz clubs, and talked elliptically in the addled voice of the addict of things they barely understood. Kerouac, like Will James, was of French Canadian descent, and he headed west with the radio tuned to the jazz stations. Ian Tyson was already as far west as he could get, and he had two choices: south or east.

"Just after I graduated, I asked my buddy, Tom Jones, to drive me out to the highway across the border. He said, 'Which way you going?' I said, 'I'll take the first one.' You could either go east over the pass or south to Seattle and Portland and on to Los Angeles."

Four Strong Winds

If I could roll back the years,
Back when I was young and limber,
Loose as ashes in the wind . . .
—("Fifty Years Ago," Ian Tyson)

A French-Canadian bootlegger from the Gaspe Peninsula who was on the lam from the RCMP stopped for Ian just north of Seattle. The Mounties had told him to shut it down for a few months, and he had been apple-picking in Washington and British Columbia. Ian rode with him two thousand miles across country to Chicago.

"I hitchhiked from Chicago to some other city and the cops ran me in. They asked me if I had any money, and they took me to the bus station. They were much more benevolent in those days. I bought a ticket for Windsor, Ontario, just across the border from Detroit, and then hitchhiked up to Toronto. Same deal—I was working within three or four days."

Ian found a job as a paste-up artist for an advertising company. Later, he designed the logo for Resdan dandruff shampoo. He got a few illustrations published, illustrations of western themes born of Will James. He arrived in Toronto without a guitar, but soon bought one— a Martin that still sits in the old line shack out behind his ranch house where he now writes. Rockabilly was dying on its feet when he arrived, but an older sound made new again was taking its place.

The birth of the Folk Boom, as it was dubbed in the late fifties and early sixties, can be traced back to one record: "Tom Dooley" by the Kingston Trio. It was the biggest pop hit of 1958, the year Ian arrived in Toronto. "Tom Dooley" was as much a pop record as it was a folk record, but folk music, like any truly ethnic music, needed to be pasteurized for mass consumption so that anything dark and unsettling could be removed. Calypso music needed Harry Belafonte; South African township jive needed Paul Simon's *Graceland*; neither could have made it on their own. If an old-timer from the Blue Ridge Mountains, where "Tom Dula" is reckoned to have originated, had walked into Capitol Records with the song, he would have been shooed back out onto the street. The Kingston Trio accomplished that much at least for folk music. They weren't folklorists or scholars; they were a close harmony pop group that caught a wave. The pop market is a crap shoot; they rolled lucky.

Ian and Sylvia on stage.

"Tom Dooley" ignited a cultural explosion. It was a phenomenon that no amount of punditry or conventional wisdom could have foreseen. By 1962, the folk boom had grown to the point where ABC television felt confident launching a weekly show, "Hootenanny." In terms of denigrating, even undermining, what it set out to celebrate, "Hootenanny" was to folk music what "Hee-Haw" was to country music. Because of "Hootenanny," or perhaps even despite it, the market for folk music deepened and widened. On one hand, there was a genuine desire on the part of some younger people for music that was both real and significant (the pop charts in the early sixties were full of music of blinding insignificance); on the other hand, it was a case study in fad-chasing.

The Kingston Trio were soon overtaken, and the most popular group to come along in their wake was Peter Paul & Mary. This was no trio of folkniks who had found their common ground in a New York coffeehouse. They had been calculatingly assembled by Albert Grossman. Starting as co-owner of the Gate O'Horn, a Chicago folk club, Grossman moved to New York and later managed Odetta, Bob Dylan, The Band, Janis Joplin . . . and Ian Tyson. The success he found first with Peter Paul & Mary typified the changing of the guard in folk music circles. They were smart, young, good-looking, politically aware, and in the way they bridged idealism and commercialism, they were very much a template for the folk singer of the sixties.

Folk music was heard in three venues: coffeehouses, clubs, and festivals. Coffeehouses had started in cities with large Italian populations and were an entirely new venue for music, adapting well to campus settings. There was the Ten O'Clock Scholar in Minneapolis, the Club 47 in Cambridge, the Troubador in Berkeley . . . and so on. The coffeehouse was the entry level for folk musicians. The next step was the folk club, like Gerde's Folk City and the Village Gate in New York, or the Riverboat in Toronto. Then there were the festivals. The pinnacle of the festival season was the Newport Folk Festival. The first, in July 1959, was produced by Albert Grossman and George Wein as an offshoot of the Newport Jazz Festival. It

"I sang to Ian first over the phone. Later, I went to meet him at the house of a lady of his acquaintance who was very upset that I was there. I was wearing brown Bermuda shorts and one of those Yugoslavian embroidered blouses which I had pinched from the costumes of the Chatham Little Theatre. Though that doesn't seem so peculiar today, Ian told me years later that it really blew his mind. I guess I was reasonably in tune, and he was interested that he hadn't heard any of my songs before. The folk singers in Toronto all worked from the same basic repertoire, because they had all bought the same records, and they were not aware of my source from books.

"Ian was fairly well established on the Toronto folk scene so he got me a job doing alternate sets with him one night a week. Then we started doing material together.

"He sang harmony on maybe one or two songs during the entire time we worked together. If he had worked at it, he could have sung harmony, but it was natural to me. My mother was an organist and choir leader in the Anglican church, and I sang parts there. From that I knew traditional harmony, but I also had an ear for creating counter-melodies."

—(Sylvia Tyson, January 1994, and interviewed in Chatelaine, January 1976.)

Ian and Sylvia in 1960 outside St. Paul's United Church, where they performed religious folksongs for a "Folklore and Religion" program.

looked certain to disappear after the riots at the jazz festival in 1960, but it reemerged as a performer-run event. Newport walked a fine line between the new, the commercial, and the traditional. Every important folk singer of every persuasion appeared there at one time or another. In the wake of the Newport festival came many others, like the Mariposa festival in Toronto.

"I started singing in the coffeehouses. Don Francks gave me my first gig. He was a very important figure—a very charismatic figure. He ran the First Floor, a jazz club on Asquith Street in Toronto. It was like breaking horses, I just blundered into it. Coffeehouses were sprouting like mushrooms all over the damn place. There were only about three or four real folk albums out then: Richard Dyer-Bennett, the Tarriers, and Bob Gibson. My main man was Bob Gibson. I just copped the Bob Gibson songs. I became an instant folk musician. I'd sing those songs in the coffeehouses, and the girls would go, 'Ohhh, that's wonderful. Did you learn that from your granddaddy?' Soon I was working every night in a different coffeehouse, so I gave up my day job. I was making fifteen bucks a night, five nights a week. A lot of money back then."

At some point in 1959, Ian Tyson met Sylvia Fricker. Sylvia was from the small southern Ontario town of Chatham, thirty miles east of Detroit. She was seven years younger than Ian. Her mother was from Ontario but had moved with the family to Michigan. She was a musician, music teacher, and amateur actress. Her father sold appliances for Eaton's, the department store chain, and was an accomplished pianist. By the age of fifteen, Sylvia had already built up a large and unusual repertoire of folk music. Always, it would always be Sylvia rather than Ian who had the abiding interest in the Anglo-Celtic forms that underpinned North American folk music.

"Our love for the music was genuine, but Sylvia was the one who searched out those esoteric songs. She had done that long before we started working together. She had a very solitary childhood. I think she felt very isolated in Chatham. If a song had a western theme, it held my interest. I started getting into the great western writers during the early Ian & Sylvia days, but I had no plans or ambitions about anything. I had no focus, no goals. No high expectations. I just tried to be good at what I did."

Sylvia commuted between Chatham and Toronto for a few months and still hadn't met Ian when she finally decided to stay in Toronto. She and Ian were introduced over the phone by Ian's employer at the advertising agency. They talked, and he offered to help her find work. Sylvia moved to Toronto in the Fall of 1959, and the week she decided to stay, she found that Ian was back west riding in a rodeo. Shortly after he returned to Toronto, he played guitar behind her on a television show taped at the First Floor; she couldn't play because she didn't have a Union card. Ian was still working as part of a duet with Don Francks and doing commercial artwork. The music Sylvia was interested in performing was very different from the then-current folk music being played around Toronto. The ballads she brought with her from Chatham had been learned from books rather than records, and she had discovered them out of an interest in literature rather than an interest in folk music.

"We were kinda like Roger Miller's 'Kansas City Star' in Toronto. We had that handled, and being young and naive, we just went to New York. Joe Taylor had the car—that was the big thing. Albert Grossman was one of the first doors we knocked on, and he said he really liked us, but he was putting together this trio, and he didn't know how much time he'd have to invest in us. We wanted to be on Vanguard Records because Joan Baez and The Weavers were on Vanguard. It seemed like the label, and we were pretty stiff-necked about it, even though Albert wasn't that keen on them. He did the deal, but he thought their emphasis was excessively on the classical side, and they didn't have a hard-nosed business attitude. He found dealing with them like trying to grab a handful of water. In retrospect, he was right."

—(Sylvia Tyson, January 1994)

"I think she hooked onto me. She had a crush on me, but after a while we developed this strange duo sound. It was based on her unique concept of harmony. I couldn't sing harmony, and on the occasions I tried, I was out-of-tune. Right to the end, she was singing harmony to my lead, and whenever we tried it the other way round, it didn't work."

Neither Ian nor Sylvia had yet started to write songs, but they put together a broad and eclectic repertoire: English and Scottish ballads, traditional American ballads, one or two French Canadian songs, several blues and spirituals, and a couple of broadsides. Then Ian & Sylvia did what few other folk singers bothered to do—and what some even thought unbecoming a folk singer—they practiced.

When Pete Seeger appeared at Massey Hall in Toronto in 1961, he put Ian & Sylvia in the audience, then called them up to sing a couple of songs. That summer, they worked at the first Mariposa Folk Festival. Ian designed the first poster. Edgar Cowan was involved in Mariposa, and he took on the job of managing Ian & Sylvia. Everyone knew that New York was the next step. Cowan wrote to twenty or so agents and record companies and lined up a few appointments. Then it was up to Ian & Sylvia themselves to go knock on doors. New York was to folk music then what Nashville is to country music now. It was where performers went to find out if they had it or maybe even to find out what *it* was. Ian & Sylvia had played every coffeehouse and folk club in Toronto more than once. They had been there and done that. It was time to move on.

"We went down to New York with a newspaperman named Joe Taylor. He was a big, big fan, and one of those guys that drove you around. Just a wonderful guy. We'd heard of Gerde's Folk City, so we went there, sang, and blew the joint up. Albert Grossman sent word to send those two Canadian kids over. He was using George Wein's apartment on Park Avenue. We went over there. He signed us. He got us a recording contract, and he sent us to the Gate O'Horn [in Chicago] for six weeks. Odetta was his meal ticket then, but he was manufacturing a trio. He already had Peter Yarrow, then he found Mary Travers, and then Noel Stookey who became Paul.

"Sylvia loved New York. She had dual citizenship, and she moved to New York before we were married. She got an apartment in the Lower East Side. I was still living in Toronto, crashing where I could. When I was in New York, I stayed at the Earl Hotel. Ramblin' Jack Elliott was there. A year later, we were all stars: Ian & Sylvia, Peter Paul & Mary. The college circuit was the big deal. That dumb television show, 'Hootenanny,' made us even bigger stars."

> "Periodically, Ian went through times of disenchantment. I think he still does. He'll fire the entire band, and everybody will go around shaking their heads. When he suggests that he sang those songs for my benefit, it's a crock. In the mid-period of our career, we chose the songs jointly.
>
> "I think Ian's attitude was something that came from his parents. They didn't have a lot of money, but they had that WASP-money attitude. My parents had the same attitude, so I understand it very well. It was the private school, the horses, going to the Lieutenant Governor's Ball with the Lieutenant Governor's daughter . . . that sort of thing. When Ian went through a period of wanting to drop out of music, I think he did it because he was never as hungry as I was. He never had to do it. He knew he had the ace in the hole. Sometime, he would come into a sum of money."
>
> —*(Sylvia Tyson, January 1994)*

Albert Grossman got Ian & Sylvia signed to Vanguard Records, the label that was already handling Odetta for him. Vanguard ("Recordings for the Connoisseur" was its slogan) had started in 1950 as the Vanguard Recording Society, a small classical label run by Seymour and Maynard Solomon. It later branched into jazz, folk, and then rock. The legendary jazz producer John Hammond worked for the Solomons for a while, and he acquired the rights to the early Newport Folk Festival recordings for the label. Vanguard signed Joan Baez after her appearance at Newport in 1959. Its name notwithstanding, the label had never been in the vanguard of anything (its fifties jazz recordings had been of thirties artists), but with acquisitions like Baez and Ian & Sylvia, it finally found itself unwittingly on the leading edge of a musical trend.

"The Vanguard secret with us and Joan Baez and Odetta was the studio. The Solomons had this place on upper Broadway called the Manhattan Towers. It was a funky old hotel, and the Solomons had discovered this room, a ballroom, a three-story interior ballroom, and they had a Neumann tape deck, a top-of-the-line German tape deck, that they placed on a little table in the ballroom, and they hung a German microphone over that. The sound was unbelievable. It was a magic room. It had a sound that enhanced and forgave. It worked until they brought drums in. The first drummer to work there was Levon Helm who was recording with John Hammond, Jr. My God, how stupid those people were. Why would you think that because you got a celestial vocal sound from this studio that percussion would work?

"The first real big breakthrough we had was at Newport in 1961. We played the main stage one afternoon. We were paralyzed with fright but apparently did well. We stuck to our guns and got a really good review in the *New York Times* from Robert Shelton, who was an important reviewer in those days. The other big breakthrough was our Town Hall concert. We got another very good review in the *New York Times* for that. That's where Bob Dylan had his first sensational solo concert. We were in that same season.

"For a couple of years, I forgot all about the west. We were going good. We had all the college concerts we could handle. On those planes every week. I bought into it for a year or two. We were making a lot of money. Ian & Sylvia was the number-two group after Peter Paul & Mary. We did two dynamite albums, *Northern Journey* and *Early Morning Rain*. That stuff wasn't manufactured.

"We sold out Carnegie Hall twice. Packed the place, but I don't really have good memories of it. We weren't practicing and weren't rehearsing very much, but the Ian & Sylvia freaks

"I think we had a romantic image with college couples who identified with us. We certainly didn't attract the crazies like Dylan. It always struck me as ironic that Dylan became a cult hero, because when we first knew him he was nervous, overweight, and penniless, and he used to hit on girls in the clubs, not to make it with them, but just to sleep on their floors. He was like a great blotter, soaking up everything from anyone who was any good, and his great talent was in the special way he put it all together. Also, he began to write his own material, and that was a revelation to everyone. We began to think, 'Hey, we can do that too.'"

—(Sylvia Tyson, January 1994, and interviewed in Chatelaine, January 1976)

accepted it uncritically. I was embarrassed by that more than flattered, but not embarrassed enough to do anything about it. I just wasn't interested. I didn't want to sing 'Nova Scotia Farewell' or 'Captain Woodstock's Courtship,' although I think Sylvia did. I liked the songs more if they had some bluegrass picking in them or if they were western-flavored, like 'Texas Rangers' or 'Molly And Tenbrooks.' In the end, we just lost our way. We never found a producer—that was part of the problem. John Court, Albert Grossman's partner, was the closest we had."

No one hanging around the New York-folk scene in 1961 and 1962 could believe what happened to Bob Dylan. Bobby Zimmerman from bleakest Minnesota took a new name from the prolix Welsh poet, a new voice from Woody Guthrie, and songs from anywhere. He possessed an infinite capacity for reinventing himself, then living the lie he had created in a very Will Jamesian way. Albert Grossman, as adept as anyone at image creation, helped to manufacture Bob Dylan from Bobby Zimmerman, then wrapped him in an enigma.

"Dylan was an obnoxious little jerk in many ways. He crashed on couches around town. He was always bummin' stuff. I never thought he'd make it like he did. He gave us a song, 'Tomorrow is a Long Time,' for our second album. Then he became so prolific when he was on amphetamines. He was just crankin' them out. He absorbed everything like a sponge. He got away with singing out-of-tune and playing out-of-tune. He got away with it, but he ain't gonna get my eighteen dollars at the door."

Between the first and second albums, Ian took his cue from Dylan and started writing songs. The second album only contained one of his original songs. Only one—but a great one.

Four Strong Winds

Four strong winds that blow lonely, Seven seas that run high,
All these things that don't change, Come what may.
But our good times are all gone,
And I'm bound for moving on.
I'll look for you if I'm ever back this way.

Think I'll go out to Alberta,
Weather's good there in the fall.
Got some friends that I can go to working for,
Still I wish you'd change your mind
If I asked you one more time,
But we've been through that a hundred times or more.

If I get there before the snow flies,
And if things are going good,
You could meet me if I send you down the fare.
But if you wait until it's winter,
It will be no good
'Cause that wind sure can blow cold way out there.

—(Ian Tyson)

"Damned if I know what the four strong winds were. I wrote it in Albert Grossman's little apartment in New York on a rainy fall day. It was basically the first song I'd written. It came real easy. The first ones always do. It was strictly autobiographical. It was about the Greek girl in Los Angeles. Now the song has become larger than life. It sounds pompous, but it has developed its own identity. Charted its own course. It's a great machine in the key of G."

Ian & Sylvia hired a bass player, Felix Pappalardi, who had been to the Juilliard School of Music. "He was quite awed that I could write these songs with three chords and one minor chord and good simple melodies," says Ian. "He always said that no amount of schooling could teach you that."

Once folk singers stopped singing the old songs, folk music gave voice to anyone crying for change—or just crying. The new generation of folk singers was heavily politicized. Dylan led the way both in and out of protest. Ian Tyson couldn't relate on the way in or the way out.

"There was a pressure on us to write or perform political songs. We were almost ostracized for not doing political stuff, anti-Vietnam stuff. I was almost non-political in those days, which is ironic because I'm very political now. I became political in my forties and fifties, but I just didn't relate then. In true cowboy fashion I just didn't relate, and it got us shut out of a lot of stuff. We did one tour in 1964 for Lady Bird Johnson with Faron Young of all people. It was a lot of fun. Then it just ended in somewhere like Fort Smith, Arkansas, and we were just stranded. We'd outlived our usefulness, I guess.

"We were living in the States, and I had a draft card, and I guess I would have gone, but I was 4-F because of the shattered ankle. I just had no concept of what Vietnam was until I went to Japan and saw these servicemen, saw on their faces that they'd been through hell."

The only political song Ian had a hand in writing was what he now concedes was a rather lame attempt to bridge the French and English solitudes in Canada. Called "Song for Canada," the lyrics were mostly written by journalist Peter Gzowski, who was from Sylvia's hometown. When Ian & Sylvia played the song at the bilingual University of Ottawa, the francophones made a point of telling them that it was already five years out-of-date. When they played the song in the United States, no one cared. So much for politics.

Folk music was changing, and in its changing form it seemed a serious alternative, even a serious threat to rock 'n' roll until January 1964. Then four Englishmen stepped off an airplane in New York, and suddenly the old rules didn't apply. Ian & Sylvia had a strong following built up by then and could still command several thousand dollars for a week's residency at a folk club. Their circuit was established, but their careers had peaked.

"The Beatles shut us down. It was over. OVER! We didn't know how to play with electric instruments. We didn't know how to use drums. We didn't know how to EQ. Then the California guys like Jefferson Airplane and the Grateful Dead came up, and they had several months on us. They'd been playing badly with amps, but at least they'd been doing it. All us folkies were just standing there with egg on our faces. The only one who had the guts to challenge the rock 'n' roll guys on their own terms was Dylan. He just jumped in.

"Even when we started trailing off, I wasn't hurting. I got the first big 'Four Strong Winds' check some time in 1963, and I went out and bought a big cattle farm east of Toronto. No one had a real big hit with the song, but everybody covered it. There were a hundred cover versions. I was out looking at the farm with Ramblin' Jack Elliott on the day that Jack Kennedy got killed. Then, in 1969, Judy Collins hit with 'Someday Soon,' and I got another big check and I bought the adjoining farm. I had 150 head of Hereford cows, and I started getting seriously into breeding cutting horses."

> "The personal relationship just evolved from being together on the road. We worked together for a couple of years before we got personally involved. Ian was cutting quite a wide swath among the local ladies on the folk scene, and I was just hanging out with friends, sitting in coffeehouses till early morning, talking. In 1964 we decided we wanted a child. We had been living together on the road, but we felt it would be unfair to the child, in terms of social and legal reasons, not to marry.
>
> "Ian was always strong-willed, and I like men who know what they want. He was always an autocrat. Self-absorbed too. I'm a little that way myself. It's part of the job description for this business."
>
> —*(Sylvia Tyson, January 1994, and interviewed in Chatelaine, January 1976).*

The cattle farm was in Newtonville, Ontario. On the same day as he went to look at it, Ian went to a rodeo held at Toronto's Maple Leaf Gardens. *Maclean's* magazine had commissioned him to write about "The Violent Art of the Rodeo." If nothing else, it showed that Ian Tyson, now at the height of his career as a folk singer still loved that damned old rodeo.

"Good rodeo riding is, like most other sports, a matter of timing," Ian wrote at the time. "The rider has to find his horse's rhythm and swing with it for the whole ride. In saddle-bronc riding, the cowboy makes a series of sweeps or 'licks' with both spurs, from the horse's shoulders back to the cantle board, a piece of wood that sticks up in the air from the end of the saddle. The licks are timed to the horse's jumps. There are about ten licks in the ten seconds he's supposed to stay onboard. It isn't just staying on that wins points from the judges, it's staying on and making your licks with some style."

Always with style.

In July 1965, a Toronto-based journalist, Jack Batten, was sent to New York to catch up with Ian & Sylvia, a local act made good. Ian told him he'd given up rodeo riding the previous summer. He'd ridden at a little rodeo in Ontario and won $18.50. "I'm never gonna cash that check," he said to Batten, "because it's the last one." The following year, he was introduced to cutting horses, light and swift quarter horses that are specially bred to separate cattle from the herd.

"I got into cutting horses through Walter Hellyer in Brantford. An old rodeo buddy of mine was training cutting horses for him. I was getting too old to ride broncs, so I got on one of these horses and it was a lot of fun. Training cutting horses is the only true cowboy sport that old guys can do. That and team roping. It's a very strange discipline. You can ride extremely well, understand the discipline very well and ride a cutting horse successfully and win in futurities, but you can also be a novice and not very good, and still ride a cutting horse, show it and win. It's difficult to know where the horse leaves off and the rider takes over. A good cutting horse does the job itself if it's well trained. The ultimate thing is doing a good job of training. Novices can show a cutting horse and win, but they can't make one. You have to be a cowboy to train one. That's what I love to do.

"I had a daughter of Doc Bar that Mr. Hellyer sold to me very cheaply. That got me in the business. Doc Bar was the be-all and end-all for cutting-horse blood. He bought five mares, daughters of Doc Bar, in California and he sold me a buckskin mare. I bred her to Buster Welch's stud, Mr. San Peppy, in Texas. I was into it pretty seriously. Cutting was experiencing a huge boom then."

"That trip to California was almost the last straw. We had a rented apartment in the middle of nowhere, and I was walking Clay around the parking lot at six in the morning, after three hours of sleep. After three or four days, I totally lost it. I hauled Clay back into the apartment, screamed at Ian. He shot out of bed like someone had thrown cold water on him, and he and Clay disappeared for the rest of the day. Clay remembers that too, even though he was very small. He and Ian had a grand old time that day, picking kelp off the beach."

—(Sylvia Tyson, January 1994)

From the outset, Sylvia made no bones about the fact that she wasn't interested in the rodeo, the cutting horses, or the farm. Ian & Sylvia was a personal and professional relationship born of compromise. After five years of performing together, they married on June 26, 1964, and bought a house in the toney Rosedale district of Toronto. Their son, Clay Dawson Tyson, was born in Toronto the following year.

It took a couple of years for the personal relationship to develop from the professional relationship. Maybe 1963. I was chasing waitresses. She had her boyfriends. Lots of them, like Tom Paxton. I know she had a crush on a New York Irish singer named Jimmy Gavin for a while. He had everything—the looks, the blarney—but he couldn't figure out folk music. Albert Grossman tried to help him, but it just didn't take. Sylvia almost never went to the farm. She was maybe there three times. She was an urban person, and she was honest about it, but, hell, you can't be a cowboy back east. People just don't accept it. They think you're an idiot or a phony. You can ride horses—but that's it. That's why Will James went west. That's why Ian Tyson went west.

"I was haying the day Clay was born. He was born with a Caesarean. There were some problems. Clay had been born by the time I got there. He was born during the last few months when Ian & Sylvia were hip. We went to California with Clay, right after he was born. They turned back our nanny, Hazel, at the border, and the trip turned into a nightmare."

Increasingly, Sylvia became disenchanted with taking Clay on the road. She realized that he would much rather be back in Toronto, and that she had tired of the road. If they took Clay with them, he would wake up early in the morning after Ian & Sylvia had been working until one or two o'clock. So, by the late sixties, they were scaling back their commitment.

Ian & Sylvia had started singing together in 1959. They gate-crashed the party in New York in 1961 and saw two good years between the middle of 1962 and the middle of 1964. The game wasn't over the instant the Beatles stepped off the plane, but from that moment all the early-sixties folkies were playing catch-up to the Beatles, or Dylan, or the Byrds, or some charlatan who came and went with one hit. Bob Dylan managed to alienate one audience, then find another. Ian & Sylvia saw their audience slowly ebb away, then tried to win over a new one. Dylan was a big noise when he changed direction; Ian & Sylvia weren't. That makes all the difference in the world when you're trying to change course.

"It came and went pretty fast. We were the hottest ticket in California for about a year and a half, and then I remember standing in a club, maybe the Troubadour in Los Angeles, and the announcer was announcing the upcoming acts, and when he mentioned Ian & Sylvia some of the people booed. That quickly we had gone from the hippest thing around to being booed. I knew there was something wrong with that audience."

Great Speckled Bird, 1973. From left to right: N. D. Smart, Buddy Cage, Ian, Sylvia, David Wilcox, and Jim Colegrove.

The Great Speckled Bird

What a beautiful thought I am thinking
Concerning a great speckled bird
Remember her name is recorded
On the pages of God's Holy word.
     —("The Great Speckled Bird,"
                    public domain)

Today "Country Rock" is the most meaningless catch-all in popular music; as pure as its original intent was, it truly signifies nothing anymore as country music edges closer to rock 'n' roll. Country-rock, as it was in the late sixties, started with several musicians who had grown up with country music and who had their heads skewed around by rock radio. Then they tried to make country music with a rock 'n' roll attitude. Many thought themselves called; few were chosen.

The pioneer was Gram Parsons, a Georgia Ivy Leaguer with a fondness for stone country music and rock 'n' roll excess. He influenced the Byrds, led by Judy Collins's ex-guitar player Roger McGuinn, to reorient themselves toward country music and record *Sweetheart of the Rodeo*. Parsons split from the Byrds before he had scarcely joined, then formed the Flying Burrito Brothers. A year later, he was out of the Burritos, off to England and hanging out with the Rolling Stones. After he came back to the United States, he recorded two albums of singular vision. In September 1973, between the release of the first and second albums, he died in a California desert motel of too much tequila and Grievous Angel Dust. The casket containing his body was stolen from the Los Angeles airport, taken back to the desert and cremated. That, apparently, had been his wish. In death, Parsons set the standard for country rock that applied until the term became so nebulous as to be meaningless.

Bob Dylan began recording in Nashville in 1966. He made it cool, even chic, to record there. His country album, *Nashville Skyline*, came a few years later—at the same time as his appearance on Johnny Cash's television show. Ian Tyson had never shared the folk world's prejudice against country music, a prejudice that was especially marked in Canada. He had grown up with country music, and had, after all, made Johnny Cash's "Come In Stranger" cut one, side one on the *Four Strong Winds* album.

Folk music as Ian & Sylvia had known and played it was dying on its feet. When they looked around, they saw Dylan recording in Nashville, and the Byrds making a token appearance on the "Grand Ole Opry," and magazines like *Rolling Stone* talking about "longhair country," so perhaps the road to Nashville was one that they could travel. The first step was a tentative one; they cut a folk-rock album in Nashville. It was called simply *Nashville*, and it was their swan song on Vanguard Records.

After Vanguard, Ian & Sylvia cut two albums in much the same vein as *Nashville* for MGM, a label to which Albert Grossman was closely connected at that time. On the cover of one album, *Full Circle*, Ian stands in his denims, looking as if he had just that minute come from his farm in Newtonville; Sylvia sits demurely at the table of their house in downtown Toronto. Much can be read into that photo—and it would probably be true.

"Grossman got us the MGM deal. He had a big bargaining chip there, and that was our last big score. Sixty- or eighty-thousand-dollar advance. Then they couldn't give the albums away.

"Parsons and McGuinn were starting this stuff, and we wanted to do it, but we crapped out. We were playing Ian & Sylvia gigs that Grossman had found for us, and we were still doing Ian & Sylvia stuff. We didn't have the guts to completely reorient ourselves. The crowds were part of the problem. Every night they wanted a faithful interpretation of the stuff they knew. That type of audience couldn't handle change. That was the audience that wanted to kill Dylan, although Dylan went out of his way to antagonize them. We should have changed our music, but we still had one foot in the Ian & Sylvia thing. We got what we deserved, I guess, which was nothing."

Great Speckled Bird was named in homage to Roy Acuff, whose signature song it was. The group's first album was released in 1969—the year after the Byrds' *Sweetheart of the Rodeo* and the same year as the first Flying Burrito Brothers album. It didn't carry the names 'Ian & Sylvia' on the front, just a curiously beheaded great speckled bird surrounded by a mosaic. It was a country rock record, though, one of the first and still one of the best. At the time, its reception wasn't negative so much as mute or nonexistent.

"Vanguard was never an aggressive record label. The Solomons' idea of an ad campaign was to put a postage-stamp-sized ad in the *Evergreen Review*. The albums we sold were due to Ian and me being out on the road, working, being visible, selling albums. With the amount we worked, if we'd had a half-way aggressive label, we could have sold ten times as many records.

"Had we gone about it in the right way we could have gone on successfully a lot longer. Ian wanted to go more and more toward a pop sound. I had no objection to it as music—I just thought we weren't very good at it. We started with *Loving Sound*, then *Nashville*. Then we were off the road for maybe six or eight months and didn't know what we wanted to do. I finally said, 'The problem is we're not a folk group any more. If we're going to tour, we have to reproduce the music we did on those albums.' Ian allowed that he'd been thinking along the same lines, and from that point we assembled the first Great Speckled Bird.

"We tried to make the band into an entity and submerge our identity into it. We were naive enough to be democratic about bands at that point—stock sharing accounts and so on."

—*(Sylvia Tyson, January 1994)*

Ian, 1974. Photograph © by Robert Gardiner.
Ian and Sylvia. Photograph © by Don Newlands.

Douglas Lake Cattle Company, 1981. (Following page)

Ian and Twylla's wedding day, August 1986. Photograph © by Gordon Biblow.

Ian and Twylla dancing at Jerry Jeff's birthday party, March 1991. Photograph by Derry Gallagher.

Tyson family, Tyson Ranch, 1991. Photograph © by Alex Pytlowany.

Twylla Tyson, Longview, 1992. Photograph © by Alex Pytlowany.

Adelita Tyson, 1991. Photograph © by Alex Pytlowany.

Ian at the N.C.H.A. Futurity, Fort Worth, Texas, 1989.
Photograph by Don Shugut.

Ian, 1987.

"We sail, and we sail together / The name of our ship is the new beginning . . ." wrote Sylvia on the back liner. "Our sails are a hopeful color / Filled with the winds of changing times . . ." The album was produced by Albert Grossman's engineer, Todd Rundgren, for Grossman's Bearsville Records and leased to the stillborn Ampex label. The album died on the vines, but it wasn't simply Ian & Sylvia's lack of commitment that scuppered it. The tape manufacturing giant, Ampex, was not set up to be a record company. Great Speckled Bird was doomed on every front.

Ian & Sylvia parted company with Albert Grossman shortly after *Great Speckled Bird*. Grossman was handling The Band and Janis Joplin and appeared to be giving short shrift to his other acts. A little later, he began withdrawing from management altogether. Janis Joplin was dead by then, The Band was disintegrating, Dylan was suing, and Peter Paul & Mary had fallen apart. Grossman stayed in Woodstock, opened a restaurant, and ran his studio. In January 1986, he died at London's Heathrow Airport en route to the music industry's annual schmooze 'n' booze fest in Cannes. He was fifty-eight.

"I don't remember how the deal with Grossman ended, so there's probably something painful there. Maybe he wasn't returning my calls. Albert really believed in Ian & Sylvia and in us separately. It has always been my wish that he could see me coming back to the corral after the big long circle. I wish Albert had seen my fruition as an artist because he believed in me."

Ian & Sylvia might have called it a day after the failure of *Great Speckled Bird*, but CFTO, the Toronto flagship station of the Canadian television network, CTV, stepped in with an offer of a show to start in fall 1969. It was called "Nashville North," a name that everyone from Ian himself to producer-director Mike Steele detested. After the first season, it became "The Ian Tyson Show," and Sylvia was a guest on fifteen of the thirty episodes a year. There was no mistaking now that Ian and Sylvia's tastes and their music were taking separate paths. In some interviews at the time, Sylvia admitted that her nose was out of joint when Ian took over the television show, but she couldn't wholeheartedly embrace Ian's shift toward country music.

"Bert Block was an old-time New York-music industry man. He and I had a falling-out over the television contract. Bert's main squeeze was Kris Kristofferson, who was hotter than a depot stove at that time. I thought Kristofferson wrote a few good songs but was otherwise a no-talent, and I never lost an opportunity to tell him that to his face, so the fact that Bert

> "Albert mistrusted and never understood television. We were the only one of his acts to do a lot of television because television in Canada was set up to showcase Canadian talent. Our contract with Albert was long over by the time of the television show. We had worked on a handshake for a while, then Bert Block, who had been Albert's partner, took over.
>
> "It was Ian's show, but they wanted me on half the shows. I knew that Ian wanted to do stuff on his own, and that was fine with me. I had Clay at home. The strange thing about that show is that back then, if they had all male artists on the show, they'd have one female artist, but if they had two female artists on the show, it was 'unbalanced.' If I was on, it would always be with the male guests. CFTO were upset that they had to do separate negotiations with me. They thought I came in a package with Ian."
>
> —(Sylvia Tyson, January 1994)

Ian, mid 1960s.

Block handled both of us created all kinds of bad vibes. It all ended when Bert sued me for back commissions based on the CFTO-TV contract. Bert was okay, but he didn't understand cowboys, and I was pretty messed-up during that time. I was not a kind person. I wasn't overly mean, but I wasn't cutting anybody any slack, because the world, the show-business world in particular, wasn't cutting me any."

Ian appeared to have decided to stand or fall with Nashville-style country music, and after the first shaky season the show consistently outdrew its only rival, "The Tommy Hunter Show," on the CBC network. The prodigal son had returned to Canada and had been rewarded with a lucrative television contract and a beer sponsorship that could, if he played his cards right, be parlayed into a new career. Ian used much of his host's fee to stock his farm in Newtonville, and he retreated there whenever he could. It was, as Sylvia always knew, a substitute for being out west. People who found Ian's unlisted phone number and called to ask if he would attend the opening of a shopping mall or a peanut festival were usually told, in unequivocal terms, where they could go.

In the early spring of 1972, journalist Bruce Kirkland was sent to interview Ian Tyson as the television show was being readied for its third season. He found a man already uncomfortable with what his life was becoming and one who seemed to draw what solace he could from the relative isolation of his farm.

"You don't interview Tyson in his Rosedale home," wrote Kirkland. "The city changes him, warps his perspective, jangles his nerves, cools his receptiveness. You talk to him perched on a bale of hay in the manure and straw-laden confines of the old barn on his 300-acre Durham County ranch.

"'I very much need this,' said Tyson, 'not for my writing, but for my head. I gotta have it. I gotta get out of Toronto. I just have to come out here as much as I can, 'cause I get too crazy when I'm in the city. I enjoy it and like it, but if I have to deal with too many people I get claustrophobic and have to split.'"

Ian's temperament was never suited to the public relations demands of a weekly television show. The show was meant to be fostering the notion that there was a vigorous and individualistic country scene in Canada, but there isn't, wasn't—and never really had been. "We imitate American music forms," Ian told Kirkland in 1972. "There are two wellsprings: black blues and white country, and that's it. The basis of both forms is the guitar. If you remove the basic American guitar forms, you'd remove everything. A lot of people say I'm American, that I sound American. Well, I probably do. I've lived down there a long time, and every singer that has ever influenced me has been American. Who would I have up here, except Wilf Carter and Hank Snow?"

That kind of bluntness didn't win friends or influence people in Canada, and the fact that it was true made it even harder to swallow.

The success of the television show kept the Great Speckled Bird band going, with inevitable changes in personnel. The band had been launched as a cooperative venture with naive sixties idealism, but the musicians that Ian and Sylvia hired inevitably saw themselves as backing men and quit, as backing men will do, as soon as a better offer came along.

"When we started, we were five of the most incompatible personalities you could imagine. We were immature as well, and didn't know how to function together. Our drummer, N. D. Smart, was a good drummer but a divisive little shit in a lot of ways. Amos Garrett was just putting his guitar style together and was experimenting in all kinds of directions. Buddy Cage was a great steel guitar player but had a little bitch of a wife who caused a lot of problems. I didn't know how to lead a band then. Now I know when to be tough, when to cut

"The station, CFTO, had the idea to bring Ian in to host the show. Maybe it was Jerry Rochon, an executive director at CFTO, who brought him in. Ian's show was conceived as a different venture from 'The Tommy Hunter Show.' We brought a lot of folk people in. Tommy Hunter was like the Lawrence Welk of country music. Ian's show was more funky, down-to-earth, people sitting down and singing. I brought in guys like Don McLean, John Prine—guys who would never get a look-in on Hunter. A lot of acts who were very *in* got on the show. Everybody was into marijuana then. They'd rehearse at the Ramada Inn down the road from CFTO, and you'd walk in and the hotel would be four feet off the ground.

"Sylvia was on maybe half the shows. It was a personal thing. It was Ian's choice—he didn't want her on the show. It was difficult then to get Sylvia to talk on-camera. She'd sing, but she didn't like to do intros. She'd say, 'Oh Mike, don't make me talk.' It was only after she'd broken up with Ian that she found she was quite capable of talking.

"I never got to know Ian that well on a personal basis. He spent a lot of time out on his farm. He didn't socialize too much with the acts after the show was over.

"The show was very popular, but Ian just decided he didn't want to do it anymore. A weekly show like that is a real commitment. I think he wanted to leave while he was on top. He thought he was going on to bigger and better things, and I think he just got tired of doing it. He was going through a tough time then. He and Sylvia were breaking up, and I know he wasn't happy here in Toronto."

—*(Michael Steele, October 1993)*

'em slack, and I've learned to speak my mind and be unequivocal. Your word has to go. One hundred percent. Back then I had no idea.

"The one thing I learned from television was how to sing and perform as a solo act. In duet singing, you throw your voice up against the other voice to get that hard, clean harmony sound that we strove to achieve. It's almost ventriloquism. Singing solo meant relearning breathing, and the television show forced me to do it because I had to learn four or five new songs a week."

Amos Garrett was replaced by Torontonian David Wilcox, a hugely accomplished guitarist who became the kingpin of the Canadian licensed venue circuit in the seventies. Buddy Cage was replaced on steel guitar by Ben Keith, a Nashville picker generally acknowledged as one of the best. Jim Colegrove was still hanging on as the bass player, and Ben Mink, lately k.d. lang's co-writer, played fiddle.

Then, unexpectedly, in 1975, Ian quit the television show. He did it on pure intuition. He put a new band together and tried to make it on his own in Canada. A&M Records signed him, and he cut a solo record, *Ol' Eon*, a record that he still ranks very highly. By the close of 1976, though, it looked very much as though another new beginning was starting to fall apart.

Over Canadian Thanksgiving, Ian Tyson looked hard at what his life had become. Ian & Sylvia were finished, although they were still technically married. Two members of his band had quit, and, as a result, he'd had to forfeit fifty-thousand dollars in bookings. The ranch was losing money because cattle prices had tumbled precipitously. A neighbor had borrowed his pickup and smashed it, the phone had been cut off because he'd neglected to pay the bill, and Sylvia's face was all over the press as her new solo record, one that Ian had produced, was hitting the stores.

"Ian and I always had different musical tastes, and we always had different tastes in terms of how we wanted to live. Through the best years of Ian & Sylvia, those differences created a tension in the music that made it really interesting. Then we reached a point where we had diverged, and it was simply difficult. It became apparent that whatever the personal relationship had been, a big part of the glue had been working together, and that no longer existed. That brought on a reassessment of the personal relationship.

"There was no last hurrah really, like The Band's *Last Waltz*. Ian wanted to put a band together and work on his own, mainly because of the television show. I wanted to be home more.

"We retained what I guess you would call an amicable relationship all through the dissolution. It was made easier by the fact that we rarely saw each other, I suppose. In some ways it was maddening for me that the harder he was to get along with, the more people thought it was part of his mystique. It got my goat because I get no slack at all."

—*(Sylvia Tyson, January 1994)*

Ian and Sylvia.

Ian's thoughts turned toward Nashville. He would have gone to the United States earlier if it hadn't been for a 1971 marijuana bust in Toronto, but, shortly after Thanksgiving, he was given a temporary visa to enter the United States and decided that it was time to take his best shot there.

"What it comes down to," he said on the eve of his departure, "is that I'm sick of being a third-rate Canadian legend. I've played in every town in this country—Moosonee, Swift Current, Gull Lake . . . you name it. It's something you have to do once. You've got to play the honky-tonks just to find out who's out there and who you're talking to. But you play the circuit four or five times, and you've got to be a fool. What does anyone want with a forty-year-old fart who won't quit? I saw Sylvia's picture in those magazines and it really pissed me off. She was starting to make it, and she wasn't even working. I was working every night in the bars and going nowhere.

"It was when the band broke up that I finally decided I had to go. I couldn't start rebuilding again. It was the best band I ever had. You can't go on writing songs about the Trans-Canada Highway forever. I've put as much into Canadian music as I've taken out. Maybe more. So I don't owe anything. And that's why I can go to Nashville and maybe never come back."

So Ian locked up his farmhouse, spent a few moments with his dog, loaded up his Cadillac, and headed for the airport. Down in Nashville, he had a manager, Melva Matthews, who had worked with Johnny Cash and Charley Pride. She had arranged for a major label to provide some seed money to record a few songs. Ian figured he could fit in with what was then called the Outlaw movement in country music. What he hadn't counted on was that the outlaws were doing the old industry schmooze every bit as much as the old-timers, and that the rebellion of most of Nashville's new breed of outlaws amounted to double-parking on Music Row.

His problems were compounded by the American Department of Immigration, which hounded him all the while he was in Nashville.

"I never got a shot because I never could schmooze. I could never pitch songs because I couldn't schmooze. That's a big part of this business. Shouldn't be—but it is. That's held me back more than anything else over the years. I've got great friends, but I could never do the industry schmooze. Industry awards—I hate them. I get claustrophobic. I want out of there. I don't see the connection between going to a cocktail party in Nashville and getting my records played in Omaha, Nebraska. Some guys, like Clint Eastwood, keep their mystique by not doing interviews. I think it's a responsibility that the record companies push off onto the artist."

Ian Tyson in Music City, November 1976

"We're heading to the Pickin' Parlor, a Nashville honky-tonk where the New Breed of Country musicians are to be found these days. Tyson had come down to Nashville hoping to join them.

"When we got there, they were already into the finale. Asleep at the Wheel had recently been nominated as country group of the year, and a lot of the right people were on-hand to help them celebrate. Most of them were up on-stage and they were singing 'I Saw the Light.' Emmylou Harris, Jerry Jeff Walker, Guy Clark, Townes Van Zandt . . . but Ian Tyson never moved. Too proud, too Canadian in his fret that the Americans wouldn't accept him, that someone would grab the microphone and say, 'Who the hell are you fella?' and some others would start laughing at this overaged galoot in the black velvet jacket. Sure, many on the stage knew Ian Tyson, but probably not many in the audience, and it wasn't a chance worth taking. Instead, he sat spinning his drink around the bottom of his glass, watching the tiny whirlpool and wishing it would suck him away, wondering if Ian Tyson finally did see the light, Lord . . .

"Emmylou Harris is standing at the other side of the table staring down.

"'Ian,' she says, 'Why didn't you come up on stage?'

"'Why,' Tyson says, his eyes shutting in a stall for time. 'Why, I'm too old. I couldn't get out of my seat.'"

—(*Star* magazine, Toronto, December 11, 1976)

Ian at Horseshoe Tavern, 1974.

Ian eventually came back to Toronto, and did the only thing he knew to do: he formed a band and started picking. Better than anyone, he knew he had nearly reached the end of the road in Ontario, and it looked very much as though he had just about bottomed out in the music business in general.

"I wanted out of music, and I wanted to be in either Alberta or Texas, but the reason I didn't go to Texas was because of the drug bust in Toronto, so they wouldn't give me a green card. I'm glad they didn't now.

"I played a date in a terrible roadhouse bar somewhere near Lake Simcoe [Ontario]. It was a horrible day. Those people didn't want me there, and I didn't want to be there. It was just awful. I just said, 'I pass.' Toronto took someone like Ronnie Hawkins [a transplanted Arkansas rockabilly whose band went on to become The Band] to its heart, but it never really took Ian Tyson to its heart. I was there a long time too.

"There was a guy from Alberta who had booked me on a couple of dates. I had a Texas steel guitar player named Tommy Spurlock, and we stayed out in the flats east of High River. We had some piddly-ass jobs, and I remember waking up and seeing the Rockies, with snow on them. I said, 'Screw it, I'd rather starve here than live in Toronto.' The Rocks have been doing that to people for 150 years."

Old Alberta Moon

*"Once I was lost
But I ain't a loser
All I need is one more hit
To stay one jump
Ahead of the Devil
These last few miles
Before I quit."*
—*("One Jump Ahead of the
Devil," Ian Tyson)*

I flew out to Alberta. I had a horse in the futurity in Fort Worth—my first or second attempt, and I was playing a rodeo in Edmonton. I took delivery of a pickup truck in Edmonton and drove all the way to Arkansas where the trainer was. We worked on the horse, then went on to Oklahoma and then on to Fort Worth. Then I drove back to Ontario. I got back in an incredible storm. I took one look at it, and I said, 'Nah. I don't need this!'

"My friend Frank Watts, he was fooling in real estate, and I said, 'Here, sell this farm.' He wouldn't believe I was going. Told me I'd be back. I had a dog, a little Australian shepherd pup, I put her in the pocket of my big coat, and me and Tommy Spurlock flew out to Calgary. We smuggled that dog on the plane. I had a big old two-horse in-line horse trailer, and Frank hitched it behind my Cadillac, and he must have made three trips. He brought all my horses, maybe about five of them, and he brought my furniture. He was a crazy guy. He brought everything out to Pincher Creek, Alberta, that summer. I placed in the Canadian futurity that fall. Frank sold my farm for a pretty good dollar. They ended up turning it into a landfill site."

Ian had hired on at a ranch in Pincher Creek where one of his buddies, Alan Young, was the foreman. He was directed toward a cabin that became home for two years. During those years, he wrote no more than two songs.

"I just shut her down. I couldn't care less about music. I just wasn't interested. I was interested in riding wild horses and chasing wild cattle. I had the middle-aged crazies. In a lot of ways, that was the happiest time of my life. The second fall at Pincher was the cattle boom. Me and Geo Brooks jumped in with both feet. We ran 1800 head of steers through the ranch. People were stealing from us and rustling, and we still made a lot of money.

"Alan had been twice around the west as a ranch foreman, bouncer . . . but nothing had jelled for him. He had legendary status as a fighter, a barroom fighter. The ranch in Pincher

Ian, 1987. Photograph © by David Gahr.

Ian and Clay Tyson, 1987.

was—and is—owned by two French Jews who were in movie distribution. They bought it as a kind of hideaway, and in Alan they discovered a guy who would party at the drop of a hat. The fact that I was a falling star had not escaped Alan, and that gave me a certain cachet around the campfire, which in turn gave me a free hand. I didn't have to worry about rent or anything. The partying was serious. There was a Friday night kickoff party, a Saturday night party, and a Sunday wind-down party. If the Frenchmen were there, it was party time four nights a week. I started avoiding the parties after a while, because I was serious about training horses."

Ian and Sylvia Tyson who had been married by the Bible were divorced by the law. Sylvia bought out Ian's interest in their Toronto house, and she stayed there with Clay.

"Clay came out to Pincher Creek a few times, and it was pretty tough on him because he'd see me with other women, and I was being pretty insensitive to it all. He was a real vulnerable kid. I don't know what his memories are. He sided with his mother, which was the right thing to do. We've never had a close day-to-day relationship since I moved out here."

After he first arrived in Alberta, Ian gave little thought to making another record. He would play dates as they presented themselves, but he thought himself finished in the record business. He was into cutting horses—not cutting records. In 1977, he fronted a band called Northwest Rebellion that played around Calgary and Saskatchewan. They did a cross-Canada tour the following year, but Ian found what he had probably always known: the music business is a merry-go-round, and you are either on it or off it—you can't jump on and off as you please.

Then, in 1978, a seed sown fifteen years earlier bore fruit. Neil Young, once a Winnipeg folkie singing "Four Strong Winds" twice a night, recorded the song for his quasi-acoustic *Comes a Time* album. Young was still selling hundreds of thousands of copies of every album, and that equated to enough for a down payment on the T-Bar-Y.

"I'd be in my cabin at Pincher Creek, and I'd know nothing about what was going on in music. I'd get a check every now and then at my mailbox in Pincher. Nothing special. But I knew ahead of time that Neil was going to cut 'Four Strong Winds' because his steel guitar player, Ben Keith, used to work for me."

In October 1978, after four years without a new record on the market, Ian issued *One Jump Ahead of the Devil* on Boot Records, an independent Toronto-area label. It was a coat of many colors stitched together from various sessions—one from Ian's abortive trip to Nashville, some from Toronto, and some finished up in Alberta. When Ian was interviewed

Nobody Thought It Would

"I wrote this with Gene Nelson, a top Nashville songwriter. We just sat down, Nashville-style, at eight-thirty, nine o'clock in the morning. He said, 'What do you want to write about?' and I started talking about Twylla, and 'Nobody Thought It Would' came out."

Stealing away to Red Deer Lake School,
A pretty young girl and a middle-aged fool,
What in the world could we have been thinking of
Nobody gave us a Chinaman's chance,
A honky-tonk romance, a tumbleweed dance
Who would have figured it would turn into love?

I have to admit we were wild as the wind
We were crazy from where they stood
But love took ahold, made a hole in our hearts
Nobody thought it would. Nobody thought it would.

Still shaking my head at the things that we did
You were trying to grow up, I was playing the kid
Summer was long with the sky-blue Rockies above
Riding pretty hard, driving too fast
Indian summer too hot to last
Who would have figured it would turn into love?

Up here the nights can get long and get cold,
I don't mind, I got you here to hold,
Big log fire, and reruns of 'Lonesome Dove,'
We don't miss a chance to have a good laugh
At the spills that we took, and the troubles we had
Who would have figured it would turn into love?

—(Ian Tyson & Gene Nelson)

Twylla Tyson on horseback with Ian in background, Longview, 1992. Photograph © by Alex Pytlowany.

shortly after the record was released, he seemed more interested in talking about the cutting horse futurity to be held in Fort Worth that December at the Will Rogers Memorial Arena.

By 1980, Ian had more-or-less forgotten about touring and the day-to-day heartache of keeping a band together, and his involvement in music was limited to regular stints at the Ranchman's in Calgary.

"The money was good at the Ranchman's. I had to make a living, but I'd be a wreck at the end of the week. I'd get out on the ranch, get my health back, then a couple of months later I'd be back at the Ranchman's. I did six, seven, eight weeks a year. I made five grand a week. That and one or two other little things kept me in horseshoes and horses. I was the only one who could get away with doing any original material there. I wrote a southern Alberta hit, 'Half a Mile of Hell.' It was a chuckwagon song. Mostly, I just did George Strait, Bob Wills, Merle Haggard. The good stuff.

"Those were the oil boom years. People were throwing money around like paper. There was drinking and fighting. Country music didn't have the younger following like it does now. It was drinking music. It was tough. Me and some others were going hard at it, trying to outdo each other in hard living."

After Ian and Sylvia divorced, Ian cut a wide swath through the available and unavailable women of southern Alberta, but he found only one who shared his vision of setting up a ranch and running it together. Twylla Biblow was a teenager when Ian met her. She worked at the Ranchman's, and had been semi-adopted by the Dvorkins, who owned the bar. Twylla was from the farming country outside Drumheller, Alberta, when she met Ian, who was then in his forties. The relationship scandalized some people at the time; few thought it would last.

"Twylla's father committed suicide. She and her brothers and sisters all had a tough time. She acted older than she was, and she got a job in a cafeteria in the Ranchman's where all the cowboys and truck drivers would go at night. The Dvorkins kinda took her in there, and she became one of their family. She lived with them all through her high school years, and then I ran her off when she was about eighteen. Alan from Pincher Creek was crazy about her, and she was crazy about him. I've often said jokingly that Alan was the great love of her life—not me. She was devastated when he died.

"I bought my ranch, and Twylla and I did a lot of the work on it ourselves. She had a job in town at a western store, and we'd spend all weekend stringing barbed wire, and riding. We trained horses, and she rode almost as much as I did. The ranch helped bring her family back together. It healed its wounds. Twylla and I didn't get married until our daughter, Adelita, was seven months old. She was born in High River Hospital in the wind, January 3, 1986. I had to leave a few days later for the second Elko. They have to have it before calving starts."

Ian's return to music came about slowly. He started by going back to the very roots of music itself: sitting around at home, playing for family and friends. What he found, after a lay-off from extended touring, was that his voice was in better shape than it had been for years. He had strained it all the years he was with Sylvia, wrestling with sub-par sound systems and trying for that elusive vocal blend; now, as he explored his voice's true highs and lows and its natural warm contours, he found that it had aged well.

"There was this Irish horseshoer I had, Noel Hope. He was a real Irishman, a real lover of the ballads. He'd get me to sing old-time cowboy stuff and Scots-Irish ballads, 'Streets of Laredo,' 'Roving Gambler' . . . all those. He was the one who started it all. He'd come out here, shoe horses, and he'd hang out. He'd come in for supper, and he'd say, 'Hoss, sing me a song with the guitar,' and I'd do it. That's what started it. And I get unhappy after a period of not writing. I need to write. That's what I do. Then I started writing the songs to get the material. *Old Corrals and Sagebrush* was done right in the house. Later, Neil MacGonigill sold the record to CBS for me."

As early as 1982, Ian was talking about his new music, and how it seemed to be coming from some wellspring within him, bubbling to the surface in a process that he didn't altogether understand. It was as if he was a conduit. "What started as a low-key informal album," he said at the time *Old Corrals* was released, "just took on its own life, its own identity. It seemed like it was recording us toward the end, rather than us recording it."

The follow-up, *Ian Tyson*, was also recorded at home, but it's an album judged by Ian and others as less successful.

"Everybody knows that is a lesser album. Year in, year out it sells one copy to four copies that other albums sell. The songs are good, 'Will James' is on there, but I produced it, and I did a shitty job. I messed up. We tried to get more electric, and some of it's out-of-tune."

Old Corrals and Sagebrush and *Ian Tyson* were western albums. "Country" and "western" had been conjoined in a shotgun wedding brokered by *Billboard*, the music trade magazine, in 1949. From that point, western music was bracketed with country music and, after a few years, the two were regarded as synonymous. The truth was that they were very different. "Country" music came from Appalachian music and was different in form and content from the song of the cowboy. The first cowboy song was recorded in 1919 when concert singer Bentley Ball recorded "The Dying Cowboy." Then, in the 1920s several authentic cowboy singers, like Jules Verne Allen and Harry McClintock, were recorded. In the 1910s and 1920s, folklorists John A. Lomax and Alan Lomax and others started to collect the songs of the cowboys, but it wasn't until the 1930s that the cowboy entered mass consciousness, and then it was through the motion picture, not the phonograph record. Gene Autry was signed to make movies in 1934, and the floodgates opened. It was Autry as much as anyone who was responsible for the confusion between hillbilly and western music, because he recorded cowboy songs side-by-side with hillbilly songs.

By the time "Country and Western" was coined by *Billboard* in 1949, western music was slowly losing out. The craze for television westerns gave cowboy music another moment in the sun, although the television theme songs were as far from the music of the real cowboy as the television westerns were from life in the west.

Leavin' Cheyenne

"Boothe Merrill, a friend of college days, gave me this song in 1910 in Cheyenne, Wyoming, where we were attending the great Frontier Days celebration. Accidentally, I had met him just as he was coming out of the saloon. He expressed surprise at seeing a former YMCA leader going into a saloon, and I expressed equal surprise at seeing him coming out of a saloon. While settling the controversy in one of the private rooms of this place, Boothe sang 'Old Paint,' which he said was popular at times in western Oklahoma. For the last dance all other music is stopped, and the revelers, as they dance to a slow waltz, sing 'Good-bye, Old Paint.' The song is yet used in western communities until the fiddler comes."

—(John A. Lomax & Alan Lomax,
American Ballads and Folk Songs)

I ride an old paint, I lead an old dan
I'm going to Montana for to throw the houlihan.
They feed in the coulees and they water in the draw,
Their tails are all matted and their backs are all raw

Good-bye, Old Paint, I'm-a-leavin' Cheyenne
Good-bye, Old Paint, I'm-a-leavin' Cheyenne,
I'm leavin' Cheyenne, goin' to Montana
Good-bye, Old Paint, I'm-a-leavin' Cheyenne.

Now old Bill Jones had two daughters and a son.
The son went to Denver, and the daughters went wrong,
His wife she got killed in a poolroom fight
But still keeps a-singin' from morning to night.

Good-bye, Old Paint, I'm-a-leavin' Cheyenne
Good-bye, Old Paint, I'm-a-leavin' Cheyenne,
I'm leavin' Cheyenne, goin' to Montana
Good-bye, Old Paint, I'm-a-leavin' Cheyenne.

And when I die, take my saddle from the wall
Put it on my pony, lead him out of his stall,
Tie my bones to his back, head our faces toward the west
And we'll ride the prairie that we love the best.

—(Arranged by Ian Tyson)

Montana Waltz

Northwest Montana sure can make her cry
Too many long nights without him,
And when Charles M. Russell gets to painting the sky,
She's all alone in the shadows.

She's much too pretty for living alone
He's much too stubborn for taming,
He's riding the range at a camp with no phone
She's all alone in the shadows.

And the wind in the sagebrush whispers him down
Whispers him down to his wintering ground,
She knows the deep snow will soon bring him down
She's gonna wait for her cowboy.

Well the last time I saw, I was workin' in the bar
Got some good bars in Montana,
Bought them a couple of rounds,
Then they jumped in his car
They were gone in the wink of his taillight.

And the wind in the sagebrush whispered him down
Whispered him down to his wintering ground,
She knew the deep snow would soon bring him down
She's long gone with her cowboy
All for the love of a cowboy.

Cover photograph for *Ian Tyson* album, 1984.
Photograph © by Jay Dusard.

It would have been tempting to pronounce western music dead, but there was always a handful of singers on small record labels who kept the legacy alive. Even then, they were recording the old songs. No one had written new western music since the thirties and forties. When Ian Tyson began writing his cameos of cowboy life in song in the early eighties, he was doing what almost no one had been doing for fifty years. *Old Corrals* also proved that he could be a masterful interpreter of vintage western songs. The style was spare and understated, and he clearly knew whereof he sang. The songs had a gritty authenticity. The romance was intact but always tempered with a stiff dose of reality.

Old Alberta Moon

It's wall-to-wall pickups in the parking lot tonight
That 'Oh, Thank God it's Friday' feeling's here,
They got a line-up at the back door,
They got three deep at the bar
Just knockin' back the shooters and drinkin' beer.

So dance the light fantastic shuffle, oh waitress smile on me,
Singers, please help me carry this old tune,
Toronto might be rhythm and blues, but if you migrate here,
You'll be howlin' at that old Alberta moon.

So gas up your Chevy, and head 'er way out west
To the land of golden opportunity
You'll get a first-hand education of how the cowboy rocks and rolls
With that old Alberta moon thrown in for free.

—(Ian Tyson)

Ian, cover photograph for *Old Corrals and Sagebrush* album, 1982. Photograph © by Jay Dusard.

Old Corrals and Sagebrush and *Ian Tyson* were placed with CBS/Columbia Records, which had no idea what to do with them. Sales pegged out around 20,000. As little as they were noticed at the time, those albums helped to set the stage for the western renaissance of the mid-to-late eighties. In those first two cowboy albums, Ian began to make the case for the vertical culture in which the North American subcontinent was divided on a north-south axis rather than an east-west axis. A song about Windy Bill the Texas man sat next to one about the Alberta ranch-hand with his Wilf Carter seventy-eights, his chores at twenty below, and "Hockey Night in Canada." An old song about the Oklahoma Hills sat next to a new one about the Alberta moon. There was no incongruity at all.

Ian at his fiftieth birthday party, September 25, 1983. Photograph © by Gordon Biblow.

Here, in the western song, Ian Tyson finally found his muse. In a broader sense, he also found what he was placed on this earth to do. Some of Ian's new songs have the epic narrative quality of the old cowboy ballads; others are wryly observed little cameos of western life. Some of the songs had the commercial gloss of Bob Nolan of the Sons of the Pioneers; others were in the tradition of the song by the nameless cowboy that somehow survived to be collected by the Lomaxes or someone else.

"The last ten years have been so weird. It's like it was preordained. It's like I was selected by something, somebody to do this. I know how changeable and difficult the journey was. When I finally got here, it was like waking up and realizing that this was the work I was always meant to do. It's scary, but it's also wonderful. Cowboy music is much freer than the folk stuff. You're not expected to do a certain song a certain way every night. There are no rules like that. It's just 'Tell me a story.'

"When it comes to horse breeding, I'd really like to go back and do it again knowing what I know now. I didn't get it right the first time. The music thing is different because I finally got it right. The funny thing is when it comes to horse breeding the knowledge is there. Guys never take it. Everyone has to learn the hard way."

Cowboys are a sub-subculture, so the authentic music of the cowboy can't be expected to sell in the millions. Columbia Records recognized that when it dropped Ian after *Ian Tyson*, but being free of a major label was more a liberation than a setback. It gave Ian the freedom to make his music that much more authentic and completely free of commercial considerations. So no one stood there more amazed than Ian Tyson when the songs he fashioned into an album in the fall of 1985 went on to become the best-selling record of his career.

Cowboyography

One fine day, says Buster Jiggs,
As he threw his cigo down,
'I'm tired of cow-piography
And I 'lows I'm goin' to town.'
—("Tying a Knot in the Devil's Tail," unknown)

Neil MacGonigill was a big believer, and he was the one who came up with the title *Cowboyography*. Was he ever right. It was a title that was just magic. Neil originally suggested the title for the album that became *Ian Tyson*, but CBS in Nashville, wonderful creative people that they are, couldn't relate to it or understand it. They thought and thought, and they said, 'We've got it! *Ian Tyson.*' I'm glad now we didn't use it for the second cowboy album, and kept it for the third.

"There's a mystical part to *Cowboyography*. I did a television show in Edmonton called 'Sun Country.' It was a fun little show. There were twenty pickers in the province and we all worked on it. I was the co-host by the second season with Dick Caldwell. They hired a new piano player, Adrian Chornowol, and he was good. Really good. Line-bred Edmonton Ukrainian. He was a classical pianist. A monster. As we got to know each other toward the end of that season, he said, 'Let me produce an album on you.' I said, 'Okay. I haven't been writing much. But I'll write some songs.' And he made *Cowboyography*. He *made* it. Then he went nuts, had a sex change. A couple of Indians knifed him. The last time I saw him, he or she was called Toby Dancer, but when he made *Cowboyography*, he was totally on top of everything. He was a genius. He had a complete vision. Arrangements. Everything. It's like he was chosen—and whoever chose him turned it off for him."

The songs were written in a cabin thirty miles from Ian's ranch, owned by a car dealer. It had the right ambiance. Just enough isolation—just enough comfort so that the songs could come.

"This cabin had electricity, plumbing, but it was isolated. Totally isolated. I went there for ten years. I wrote five albums there. I'd go there at seven thirty, eight o'clock in the morning. I'd come back at one in the afternoon, and I'd start training horses. I got to know a little black bear and a mother moose up there. I'd see them for years."

Some songs have to be teased out line-by-line, but on *Cowboyography* even more than on the first two cowboy culture albums, the songs flowed, almost presented themselves to Ian. The song that everyone remembers often comes to the writer in a matter of minutes. It may be tarted up later, but the essence comes in minutes. The great songs are like chimeras that the

The Tyson cabin. Photograph © by Gordon Biblow.

songwriter must catch before they disappear. The antennae must be up to receive them.

"I was in the cabin. It was snowing, then there was a chinook. I woke up in the middle of the night in a dreamlike state, and the songs were just there. In the morning, I woke up and realized that something was going on here. Something beyond my control. That's how it always is when you do your best writing. You get that adrenalin rush and you can finish the song. Eight times out of ten it's in the morning. By one o'clock, it's gone. If you get an idea at night, you'd better get up and write it down 'cause it'll be gone by morning. Hard work and inspiration overlap. Your knowledge of the craft will let you take advantage of inspiration."

Ian was now off CBS/Columbia and didn't have the funds necessary to record *Cowboyography* in the way that Chornowol wanted, so he bankrolled the album through two friends, car dealer Einar Brasso of Calgary and rancher Dan Lufkin from New York City and Prairie City, Oregon. It cost $37,000, about one third the cost of the cheapest major label country record made today. It was released in November 1986, and Ian and Twylla began selling it via mail order on their own Eastern Slope Records. At the same time, it was handed over to the Edmonton-based Stony Plain label for mainline distribution in Canada. Initial sales were spurred by a few months' solid airplay of "Navajo Rug" in and around Calgary.

Cowboyography was one of those times when the unknowable happened. All the stars were in alignment, just as they had been when Ian scribbled out "Four Strong Winds" in Albert Grossman's apartment. The new songs formed a tapestry of life on the eastern slope, and, in a broader sense, the west. If anyone had set out to write a song cycle about life in the west today, it would have emerged stilted and self-conscious, just as no one writes the great American novel by sitting down with the intention of writing it. *Cowboyography* started with very limited goals. It was to be a small record, aimed at those who would understand all the references and allusions in the eleven songs. Then it took on another life and became a mosaic of western values and emblems. What was meant to be heard by a very limited number of people ended up being heard by over one hundred thousand.

"I never cared if *Cowboyography* was heard by anybody other than the 700 working cowboys in North America," said Ian at the time. Asked to explain its success, he was clearly at a loss. "There's got to be a fad aspect to this. There has to be. I'm singing subculture music for an audience that's gotten much bigger than the subculture. I just wanted to be the voice of the cowboys, the working cowboys, because those guys can't relate to the Nashville urban cowboys. I just wanted to speak for them. I didn't know it was going to get out-of-hand."

Cowboyography was in many ways an anti-Nashville album. Ian made the distinction in an interview he gave shortly after it was released. "Those people in Nashville aren't writing

Springtime

Ian at the Whitehorse Ranch, 1984. Photograph © by Kurt Markus.

"I wrote 'Springtime' in the cabin that time when it chinooked and it went up sixty degrees overnight. The water was running like crazy. It drowned a bunch of cattle."

Bald eagles back in the cottonwood tree
The old brown hills are just about bare,
Springtime sighing all along the creek
Magpies ganging up everywhere,
Sun shines warm on the eastern slope
March came in like a lamb for a change.
Gary's pulling calves at the old stampede
We made it through another on the northern range.
Well, the big chinook blew in last week
Warm and strong from the western sea,
Pretty soon water running everywhere
Hell, it couldn't run fast enough for me.
Broodmare's sleeping in the afternoon sun
She's shedding hair everywhere—time for a change,
George is pulling calves at the T-Y
We made it through another on the northern range.

Bald eagles back in the cottonwood tree
The old brown hills are just about bare,
Springtime sighing all along the creek,
Magpies ganging up everywhere.
Sun shines warm on the eastern slope
March came in like a lamb for a change,
Larry's pulling calves at the Quarter Circle S
We made it through another on the northern range,
Larry's pulling calves at the Bar 4 Orlock
We made it through another on the northern range,
Jean's pulling calves at the Horseshoe Bar
We made it through another on the northern range,
Ian's in the hills trying to write songs
God's in the country where the tall grass grows.

—(Ian Tyson)

Ian at the Calgary Stampede, 1979. Photograph by Walt Browarny.

songs about cowboys," he said. "They're writing about rural people who have been screwed up by city life." Even so, there was no sidestepping the commercial reality that if *Cowboyography* was to be played on radio, it would be on country stations. But then, as if to reinforce the notion that the stars were truly in alignment for *Cowboyography*, it came at a time when a curve was thrown into the oppressively tight formatting of country radio. Early in 1986, Randy Travis, Dwight Yoakam, and Steve Earle all appeared on the scene, and the catchphrase "New Traditionalism" was on everyone's lips. Ian Tyson caught a wave, much as he had twenty-five years earlier. His music fit in curiously well with the old sounds made new again.

Not all the songs on *Cowboyography* were new. "Old Cheyenne" came from the *You Were On My Mind* album back in 1972, and "Summer Wages" finally found its true home on the third go-round. It had first appeared on *So Much for Dreaming* in 1967, and then on *Ian and Sylvia* four years later. Of all the songs on the album, it was perhaps the most universal. It was the plaint of the joe on the joe-job, his money quickly spent, feeling the need to move on.

Cowboyography also contained Ian's hymn to Charlie Russell, the great western painter. Like Will James, Charlie Russell wasn't from the west; he was born in St. Louis, Missouri, in March 1864. His father owned part of Parker-Russell Mining and Manufacturing. Charlie left for Montana shortly after his sixteenth birthday. A friend of his father's owned a ranch in the Judith Basin, and Charlie hired on. He wasn't much of a cowboy, not even much of a night herder, and the only time he ever outrode the cowboys was in the race to the cathouse, but if he had been a better cowboy he would probably never have been the painter that he was.

Russell's experience and the political philosophy he developed from it, find their direct parallel in Ian Tyson. Russell became almost desperately averse to change. He wanted to freeze the west circa 1888, the year before Montana became a state. His conservatism, like most

Summer Wages

"In those days, there was always work. A lot of guys would hole up in the wintertime and wouldn't work, and they'd live on summer wages. The summer was when you would make your score. It was about loggers more than anything. These days, they often shut down the forests in summer because of the fire hazard."

Never hit seventeen
When you play against the dealer
For you know that the odds
Won't ride with you,
Never leave your woman alone
When your friends are out to steal her,
Years are gambled and lost
Like summer wages.

And we'll keep rollin' on
'Til we get to Vancouver
And that woman I love
Who's living there,
It's been six long months
And more since I've seen her,
Maybe gambled and gone
Like summer wages.

In all the beer parlors
All down along Main Street
The dreams of the seasons
Are spilled out on the floor,
All the big stands of timber
Just waiting for falling,
And the hustlers
Standing watchfully
As they wait by the door.

So I'll work on the towboats
With my slippery city shoes
Which I swore I would never do again,
Through the great fog-bound straits
Where the cedars stand watching
I'll be off and gone
Like summer wages.

—(Ian Tyson)

Ian at his ranch, March 1984. Photograph © by Jay Dusard.

conservatism, was born of privilege, but in Russell's case the privilege was that of seeing the unfenced range and the absence of settlement. He was fond of telling how, when he returned home to St. Louis for the World's Fair in 1903, he passed by all the exhibits dedicated to progress and instead spent time with a caged coyote who, he said, "licked my hand like he knew me, I guess 'cause I brought the smell of the plains with me."

Everyone, Russell said, wants to be the last one into the west, and he was curmudgeonly in his desire to deny future access, even roll back the clock. "I wish to God," he told a

Montana booster gathering, "that this country was just like it was when I first saw it, and that none of you folks was here at all." He empathized with the plains Indians who lived in harmony with nature and had no desire to overrule it, and his drawings and paintings of them weren't crude caricatures but were suffused with dignity.

Something of Russell can be gleaned from a letter, written six years before his death to Will James. "Use paint, but don't get smeary let somebody elce do that keep making real men horse and cows of corse the real artistick may never know you but nature loving regular men will and thair is more of the last kind in this old world an thair the kind you want to shake hands with . . ."

The Gift

In old St. Louis over in Missouri,
The mighty Mississippi it rolls and it flows,
A son was born to Mary Russell
And it starts the legend every cowboy knows.

Young Kid Russell he was born to wander
Ever westward he was bound to roam,
Just a kid of sixteen in 1880
Up in wild Montana he found his home.

God made Montana for the wild man
For the Peigan, the Sioux and Crow,
But He saved his greatest gift for Charlie
Said, Get her all down before she goes, Charlie,
You gotta get her all down 'cause she's bound to go.

God hung the stars over Judith Basin
God put the magic in young Charlie's hand
All was seen and all remembered
Every shining mountain, every longhorn brand.

He could paint the hide on horsehide shining
Great passing herds of the buffalo
And a cowcamp cold on a rainy morning
And the twisting wrist of the Houlihan throw.

When the Lord called Charlie to his home up yonder
He said, Kid Russell, I got a job for you
You're in charge of sunsets in old Montana
'Cause I can't paint them quite as good as you,
And when you're done, we'll go out and have a few,
And Nancy Russell will make sure it's just two."

—(Ian Tyson)

Ian Tyson and Tom Russell, 1988, New York City. Photograph © by David Gahr.

The hit on *Cowboyography* was "Navajo Rug," a song Ian had written with Tom Russell. Most of Russell's songs are too long and too prolix for Nashville and country radio, but, reined in by Ian's songwriting discipline, the two came up with something radio learned to love.

"When I was really out of the music in the summer of seventy-nine, Twylla and I were at a cutting horse meet in Montana, and it was really hot—high nineties. I was blowing everybody away with the horse's big moves, but I was making little errors and wasn't getting marked. This guy came over, and he said, 'You're a non-pro. Did you train that horse?' I said, 'Yeah.' He said, 'That was spectacular.' We got to talking and he asked if I was the same Ian Tyson that was with Ian and Sylvia. He said, 'My name's Dan Lufkin,' and he asked me if I still had a band, and I told him I did—occasionally. Then he asked me if I'd come back to New York to play his twenty-fifth wedding anniversary. I said, 'Sure.' I charged him $2500 plus expenses. We went, and we had a ball.

"I phoned Tom Russell, told him we were coming to New York. When he was a kid he was a fan of mine. When we were the thing in California, Tom heard us there. He was in the Peace Corps in Africa and had a bad time. He came back and started writing songs, and he sent me 'Gallo de Cielo.' Nobody would touch him in Nashville—they listen to him at home, but they don't cut him, but I liked his work and I cut it, and 'Gallo' became a kinda underground classic. We kept in touch, but I couldn't believe the guy that wrote the songs he did lived in Brooklyn. I went out to this slum he lived in. Puerto Rican guys standing around giving you the once over, and there was old Russell on the corner laughing away. He took me to the bunker. We got out the wine, and we said, 'We got to write a song.' I asked him what he had going, and he didn't have anything, but he said, 'What do you think of a song about making love on a Navajo blanket?' I said, 'Wow, yeah. What a great image. Let's write it.'

"We finished it on the phone. I was in the Super 8 motel just off I-30 in Fort Worth, and he was back east somewhere. He wrote the verses, I wrote the chorus and the melody. It was entirely fictitious as far as I know, but it was a very important song on *Cowboyography*. A huge radio song."

Navajo Rug

Well it's two eggs up on whiskey toast
Home fries on the side,
Wash it down with roadhouse coffee
Burns up your inside,
It's a canyon, Colorado diner
And a waitress I did love,
I sat in the back 'neath an old stuffed bear
And a worn out Navajo rug.

Now old Jack the boss, he left at six
And it's, 'Katie bar the door'.
She'd pull down that Navajo rug
And she spread it on the floor,
Hey, I saw lightning 'cross the
    sacred mountains
Saw woven turtle doves
When I was lying next to Katie,
On that old Navajo rug.

Aye, aye, aye, Katie,
Shades of red and blue
Aye, aye, aye, Katie,
Whatever became of the Navajo rug and you?

I saw old Jack about a year ago,
He said the place burned to the ground,
And all I saved was this here old bear tooth
And Katie she's left town,
But Katie, she got her souvenir too,
Jack spit a tobacco plug,
You shoulda seen her coming through
    the smoke
With that old Navajo rug.

So every time I cross the sacred mountains
And lightning breaks above,
It always takes me back in time
To my long lost Katie love,
But everything keeps on a moving
And everyone's on the go,
You don't find things that last anymore
Like an old woven Navajo.

Aye, aye, aye, Katie,
Shades of red and blue
Aye, aye, aye, Katie,
Whatever became of the Navajo rug and you?

—(Ian Tyson and Tom Russell)

Ian at his ranch, 1987. Photograph
© by Kurt Markus.

Ian at his ranch, 1986. Photograph © by Kurt Markus.

Cowboyography was the complete package. Kurt Markus's photos were the clincher. In them, Ian looks frozen as if in an 1880s daguerreotype. The front cover photo had an immutable stillness that echoed back to the time when people would stand motionless for seconds to have their image engraved, as if to reemphasize a slower, measured pace of life. Like the music, the jacket had an elemental simplicity that said more with less.

Jay Dusard, who took the photos for *Old Corrals and Sagebrush*, and Kurt Markus were integral to the cowboy renaissance for which *Cowboyography* was the soundtrack. Both Dusard and Markus shared Ian's quest to separate the spurious from the authentic and capture what was real before it was gone.

"The first photographer was Bank Langmore. He was a good commercial photographer, and some institution or other wanted some cowboy photos. Big colorful ones. Bank is a fanatical guy. When he gets the bug for something, he goes nuts. He discovered cowboys—he didn't come back for three years. He went out with the wagons. He wasn't one of these guys who photographed cowboys from the road in his rental car. His book, *Cowboy*, came out and made a big stir. He went to some great old outfits. A lot of them are gone now. He went to these outfits where every buckaroo on the place was wanted. The FBI wouldn't go in without a SWAT team.

"Then came Dusard. While we were doing *Old Corrals*, Neil MacGonigill saw these incredible photos Dusard had taken that were on exhibition in Calgary. He said, 'God, you've got to see this stuff.' And it was so fresh and new. Neil said, 'I'm gonna call this guy, get him to come up and take your album cover.' We did the session in the barn and the feedlot.

"And then came Kurt Markus. Dusard and Markus were very important in the cowboy renaissance because they took pictures of a lost world. Markus took it further than anybody. He took it to the max. If they were going to ride sixty miles that day, he'd ride the sixty miles. Markus took me with him on some of his trips into Nevada. Nobody knew about these places. We went to a camp where they had hidden Claude Dallas. We went to the White Horse, and damn if they weren't putting in a satellite dish the day we came. God, that was an isolated place. It makes my spread look like suburbia. It's in a black hole on the map, two hours from McDermitt, a little Indian town on the Nevada-Oregon line with a bunch of slot machines, a gas station, and two bars. All the guys on the White Horse packed guns."

Cowboyography was, as Ian says, a real vindication. The record industry had written him off, and the supposition had always been that it was their way or no way.

"It didn't really hit me until I started winning the awards. The Canadian Country Music Association awards were in Vancouver, and I won about five awards. That's when it sunk in. Up till then, I'd never won an award. It was like it was against the law. I still think *Ol' Eon* was a great album, but every year by rote Stompin' Tom Connors was handed the Male Singer, Album of the Year . . . whatever. *Cowboyography* broke the log jam."

Word about *Cowboyography* spread. It not only coincided with a new wave in country music, but also with a renewed awareness of western American culture as a thing apart from the mainstream of American culture. At its root was a sense of pride in a culture forged of necessity. Folklorist Hal Cannon started a cowboy poetry gathering in Elko, Nevada, in January 1984. His underlying assumption was that everyone else had told the story of the cowboy, and no one was buying it anymore, so perhaps it was time for the cowboys, the working cowboys, to tell their own stories before every ranch had a satellite dish and every camp had a cellular phone.

"Elko is more folk music than anything I ever did when I was a folkie. It's real folk music. Those guys, they're not all cowboys—there are some wannabes, but it's the real thing. I'm a product of Elko in terms of my American following. It was supposed to be real cowboys and not professional entertainers, but they wanted me, so they got me the gig at the casino. I blew the place apart. Then everybody wanted to come, Jerry Jeff Walker, Michael Martin Murphey, and they tried that for a couple of years. Now they've shut it down. The music got bigger and bigger at Elko, pushing the poetry aside. They were worried about that, and they've started their own music festival in the summer. I headlined the first one. Music is so strong in the world today that it just shoulders aside the poetry.

"There hasn't been a Bob Dylan of cowboy poetry. The Bob Dylan of cowboy music has been me, but no young genius has come along and revolutionized cowboy poetry. It would have to be a real cowboy for it to work. It's still based on Bruce Kiskaddon and Charles Badger Clark—the old stuff. Nobody makes any real money at it, except maybe Waddie Mitchell who's on 'The Tonight Show' every now and again. Baxter Black does well too. He knows how

"Cowboy poetry survived the cowboy hype of the sixties. It just went underground. These new stories don't have as much to do with social justice as the old ones. They have much more to do with an agricultural reality, making a livelihood in the open places, rather than the Arthurian stories. We've just helped to bring it to a wider audience. Sure, the culture is under a lot of pressure, but that's when the expression of a culture comes out most vividly.

"We've never really put a big emphasis on music at the poetry gathering. We spent our first grant money on bringing in poets, and that's what we've always tended to spend our money on. The first year, we didn't have any money to bring Ian in, but I wanted him, and I thought the cowboys would like him, so I went to a casino, the Red Lion Inn, and told them we'd rent a bunch of hotel rooms if they booked Ian. We booked all our rooms there, then they called and said they'd booked a band for the night Ian was supposed to play, so I pulled all the room reservations and took them to another casino where they would hire Ian."

—(*Hal Cannon, 1994*)

to market himself. Hell, I learned from Baxter. In the regional gatherings, they still mix the music and the poetry. The sessions afterward were like folk music was supposed to be. They get out the guitars and banjos. They just go all night long. They're not that good, but they do it for fun.

"Cowboy poetry might even have died out without Elko; or it might just have hung on in Nevada and eastern Oregon. You have to have real isolation for cowboy poetry."

Hal Cannon doesn't agree that Elko was critical to the survival of cowboy poetry; quite the contrary, he sees technology as an aid to its survival. Cassettes are circulated, and what was once an underground tradition comes above ground. At the same time there is the reinforcement necessary to keep the tradition flourishing. The only virtue of isolation, says Cannon, is that it leads to more variety of expression. Once you could tell where a cowboy came from by his hat or his talk; now it's more homogeneous.

Performing at Elko, Ian experienced that moment of epiphany as a performer that had more-or-less eluded him even when he was at the top of his game with Ian & Sylvia. The audience was comprised of his people. They related to everything he said and were at the heart and soul of everything he was singing about. Up on stage in front of them, Ian no longer felt his age, his aches and pains, or the frustration of trying to reach out for a crowd that can't be reached. He finally achieved that moment of holy communion between performer and audience that is the stuff of performers' dreams.

Ian Tyson, Hal Cannon, Kurt Markus, and Jay Dusard all became aware of each other at roughly the same time and realized that they were all approaching a common goal from different directions and different perspectives. Elko was the focal point that brought everyone together and gave focus to what became known as the Cowboy Renaissance.

Cowboyography was followed by *I Outgrew the Wagon*, a collection that reaffirmed and reworked the same themes. On the cover, Ian ventured a smile under the big, big sky. It was tantamount to contentment. The song that attracted radio play was "Irving Berlin (Is 100 Years Old Today)," an allegory on the western drought that seemed to be on the point of turning the clock back to the pestilential years of the thirties.

Irving Berlin
(Is 100 Years Old Today)

"I was up on the far fence line. I was listening to Peter Gzowski's 'Morningside' on CBC on the truck radio, and they made mention of Irving Berlin's hundredth birthday. It was one of those magic moments. The song just presented itself. Irving Berlin didn't have much to do with it. A lot of people don't relate to it. It's like an abstract painting. You get out of it what you want to get out of it. The radio is a stream-of-consciousness thing. You only half-listen."

I started them fillies at the pens this mornin'
You know the buckskin and the bay,
Before the wind started blowin' too hard
At the mid part of the day,
The driest spring in ninety-one years
The radio played on.

The Bay's a little sweetheart . . . yeah she is
Pretty much like her mom,
The Buckskin's rank . . . took me twenty minutes
Just to put the hobbles on,
She's smart and she's fast and she doesn't like people
She trembles as she stands.

Irving Berlin is a hundred years old today
The wind's gone and blown my woman away.

Good Gawd a'mighty is it ever gonna rain?
Are you ever coming home?
I wonder if Irving Berlin ever wrote a song
About blowed out country, a marriage gone wrong
And a cowboy on the telephone?

Irving Berlin is a hundred years old today
The wind's gone and blown my woman away.

Happy birthday, Irving, God bless you
Are you glad just to be alive?
The hockey game is on tonight from Boston
I've got the Oilers in five,
Tomorrow I'm gonna try and fix this tractor
And try to keep my mind off-a-you.

Irving Berlin is a hundred years old today
The wind's gone and blown my woman away.

—(Ian Tyson)

Ian and Tom Moon at the 1989 Edmonton Folk Festival. Photograph © by Peter Sutherland.

The fifth chapter of Ian's cowboy culture albums was *And Stood There Amazed*, a title taken from a line of "Home On The Range." It's a song that everyone knows—and no one knows. The first verse and chorus are among the most familiar in American popular music; the second and third verses, which hold the song's poetry, magic and true meaning, are known only to a few:

> *How often at night when the Heavens are bright*
> *With the light from the glittering stars,*
> *Have I stood there amazed, and asked as I gazed*
> *If their glory exceeds that of ours.*

"Anyone who lives out on a ranch where there's no pollution and there's no glow from any city can relate. You can walk out on your porch on any clear night and you're just astounded by the heavens. Millions of people don't see those skies anymore. You really do stand there amazed. That line was so appropriate."

The success of *Cowboyography* and *I Outgrew The Wagon* presented their own problems. Ian was quite suddenly pitched into the role of spokesperson for the cowboy revival. His thirty years in front of an audience meant that, on one level at least, this presented no problem, but on another level he resented the loss of privacy as well as the way he seemed to be on the edge of being co-opted by the very commercialism to which his lifestyle and albums were now desperately opposed.

Ian, 1991. Photograph © by Alex Pytlowany.

Photograph © by Ellen Brodylo and Mike Morrow, 1987.

Cowboy Pride
Ten Years Later

Oh give me a home where the buffalo roam
And the deer and the antelope play
Where seldom is heard a discouraging word
And the skies are not cloudy all day . . .

—*(Dr. Breweter Highley)*

They've been selling the west since Buffalo Bill. At the beginning of this whole cowboy renaissance thing, they had the idea of bringing it to the world, packaging it up, getting real Disney. It didn't happen, and I don't think it's going to. I don't think you can take it out of the West."

For Ian Tyson, it's a matter of pressing concern now that the last vestiges of untrampled western landscape and unadulterated western culture remain preserved. The neutering effects of urbanization, suburbanization, and corporatization are irreversible, and they go hand in hand with uniformity and conformity. Over and above that, there's a spiritual malaise that has created a neurotic rootlessness. There's a sense of wanting to get back to the land to recover a misplaced sense of identity in a mythic past, but no one quite knows where to go to do it. The west seems the best bet, but in the very act of going, the last of what's left is destroyed.

In the arc of opinion about the future of the west, Ian holds one of the bleaker perspectives. The interest and attention focused on the west will, he contends, be its undoing.

"The west in that wild sense has gone now. The wind is still here, the sky is still here, the Rockies are still here, and the light—that western light—is still here. The ecosystem is still here—the deer, the bears wandering up from the river, wolves, geese screaming at you. There's still lots of space, but it's going fast. Everybody wants to be the last one in. You can't blame them.

"The weekend ranchers will change the character of the landscape. The open country will just disappear. It's still big—but it gets smaller every year. It's selfish. I want this for

Twylla, Adelita, and Ian, 1991. Photograph © by Alex Pytlowany.

Adelita, age six. Photograph © by Gordon Biblow.

Rocks Begin to Roll

Open wide the gate, boys
Let my ponies run,
I'm going to travel on the gravel
Head her for the setting sun,
Give me sixteen broncs unbroken
Out on the eastern slope,
Truck 'em all the way from Oregon,
Leave me there to cope.

Way out back in the back of beyond
Where the nights are dark as coal
And the circle stays unbroken
And the rocks begin to roll."

—(Ian Tyson)

myself. Open country is intrinsic to the culture of the west. You can't have it in twenty-acre parcels. We cling to the real thing, but at the same time I'm part of the problem because I'm selling the west, causing more people to move here than anybody."

The cowboy culture is as integral to the west's sense of apartness as cotton and the culture that attended it once were to the south. At Elko, Ian began to sense that his music might be more than a Christmas card to a few friends and fellow believers. It reinforced his view that living and working as a cowboy had more importance than simply sustaining a childhood dream that had been nourished by a French Canadian calling himself Will James.

"There are ranches that make a very conscious, serious effort to run in the traditional way. The cowboy on horseback. You can run a ranch with helicopters, three-wheelers, baseball caps, but the traditional way is better. It's a better way of handling livestock in open country. It's just better, but you have to have the guy with the skills. You can't just put a cowboy hat on a guy and put him on horseback, but a lot of guys work very hard at maintaining the skills. Cowboys want to look good while they're doing what they do. That's important to them. It has to be done with a lot of style. Cowboying isn't something that's been preserved artificially from a hundred years ago like a lot of people in the east probably think. There is a reason for it.

"With a cowboy, you have the freedom that we're all looking for—then you put it on a horse. The man on the horse. Man changes when he's on a horse, and when he's on a good horse, he really changes. A good horse liberates you. I ride across the hills under the moon. It's magic. You're on a living machine that eats up the miles. It's a tradition that crosses borders. Look at the gauchos and the vaqueros, Genghis Khan, the Cossacks . . ."

Canada, with its social safety net, discourages cowboy self-reliance. Everyone's a professional victim now, too. There's no need to strive for anything because the state will pick you up every time you fall down, and an army of psychobabblers are waiting to tell you that you're not responsible for yourself or your problems. Ian was courted by the Reform Party, a Calgary-based party that stands—among other things—for less government, less handouts, less immigration, less of all the things that have sapped cowboy pride. They wanted him to stand in the federal election of 1993. He didn't, although he often finds himself in sympathy with them.

"I was born on the wrong side of the border, I guess, like Will James. A lead guitar player I just fired was from Maryland, and I used to tell him, 'You're a real Canadian. You were born on the wrong side of the border.' He wanted to be taken care of all his life—which is why he got fired. I used to tell him, 'I was meant to be born in Wyoming, and you were meant to be born right here in the middle of the social safety net.'"

For all the success of *Cowboyography*, the commercial fate of western music still rests with Nashville. There's more western music being made than at any time for decades, but very little in the way infrastructure has grown up to support it. Nashville once chewed up cowboy music and left it for dead and always holds out the promise of doing the same thing again.

In 1991, Warner Bros. Records sensed a groundswell of interest in western music after the unexpected success of Michael Martin Murphey's *Cowboy Songs*, and it started a Warner Western imprint. At the same time, Garth Brooks did a duet with cowboy singer Chris Ledoux, and suddenly, in Garth's reflected glory, LeDoux was on Capitol's Nashville label as well. Nashville only extends its embrace to the salable, so it seems that the lure of the cowboy is still very much alive. At the same time, what is real and different about western culture is on the point of being subsumed to commercial interests again. The song of the cowboy is being co-opted to add a few dollars to Music City's already bloated bottom lines.

Ian is ambivalent. On one hand, he is as innately conservative as Charles M. Russell

> "The marketeers will always try to take over. People seem to be reaching back into their most familiar pocket and finding these cowboy images that were tired in the fifties and sixties, and that's why people gave them up. Now they're being dragged out again to satisfy people's interest in stories from the rural west. I for one don't want to play into it."
>
> —*(Hal Cannon, 1994)*

ever was and has a profound mistrust of the entertainment business that he has nurtured over the last thirty years. On the other hand, he knows that Nashville can make the difference between a few thousand people buying his records in the United States and a hundred thousand or more. Back on Vanguard Records, ironically now a subsidiary of Lawrence Welk Music, he recorded *Eighteen Inches of Rain* in Nashville.

"I was apprehensive about recording in Nashville. Country music is the rock 'n' roll of the nineties; it's what redneck kids are listening to. It's got nothing to do with what I do. We went to a Dwight Yoakam concert in Calgary and it was a Canadian audience like I'd never seen before—or since. It was an amazing night. Suzy Bogguss was on the bill and she wanted me to sing with her on 'Someday Soon,' and I did. That place was jammed. The energy was incredible. They were yelling for Yoakam twelve or fifteen minutes before he ever came on. I've never seen that in Canada.

"Nashville has a stranglehold on radio, and I don't relate to what they do. They don't want to play sixty-year-old guys; they want to play twenty-two-year-old guys. On one level I admire Nashville songwriting. They go in the morning, and they have to write what's called 'personal relationships.' They can't write knife and whore songs like Tom Russell. Almost half the songs on *Eighteen Inches of Rain* are collaborations. I'd only ever collaborated before with Russell, but this is professional Nashville-style collaboration. I just brought the cowboy sensibility to it."

When Ian went to record *Eighteen Inches of Rain*, he was paired with producer Jim Rooney, who had been a folk music booking agent in the sixties, and had, at one time, written a book on Muddy Waters and Bill Monroe.

"Rooney was the right producer. It was Pat Alger's recommendation, and was he ever right. Jim and I had known each other for thirty years, but we'd never worked together. He and I are both late bloomers. He was low-key but all business. We did it Nashville style. We cut two bed tracks [backing tracks on which the vocal is overdubbed] in the morning and two in the afternoon. An awful lot of that album is live right off the studio floor. I think that's why it has freshness and immediacy. Nothing went over three takes. Jim and I played the demos for the pickers to show them what we wanted, and they treated it like a road map—just tried to make it a little better and a little smoother. We cut the album in less than a week. It wasn't glamorous but it worked.

"The pickers were fascinated with the songs, loved them. They wanted to know what some of the cowboy terminology meant. It was different for them, and they really enjoyed it. They were focused but in a nice, relaxed way. There were no technical delays. It was a far cry from 'Let's finish this and get stoned. Let's get some whores in here,' like it was twenty years ago."

Eighteen Inches of Rain

"Pat Alger and I wrote this. Pat is a fan, and he believes strongly in putting stuff back in the business. He does songwriting workshops, and he did one in Vancouver for [the performing rights organization] SOCAN, and he asked if there was any chance of me coming out there, and I asked him out here. We wrote this song in the cabin. It took a day and a half. Pat was so hot, you couldn't put your finger on him."

Not a broke horse on the place,
Pickup truck won't go,
Tractor lost a wheel 'bout a week ago,
Wind is from the east,
Blowing hard across the plains
High and lonesome, waiting for a change.

Coffee's kind of bitter
Is it the water or the pot?
Until I get to town
I'll make do with what I got,
Copenhagen's running low—should quit it anyways,
Me and this outfit—we've both seen better days.

Give me one broke horse,
With a good-fitting saddle
That's easy on your back,
One good woman who makes the difference
For everything I lack,
One last chance to sell my calves
Before the price goes to hell again,
Clear blue skies, and eighteen inches of rain.

— (Ian Tyson & Pat Alger, Slick Fork Music/
Forerunner Music/Bait & Beer Music)

Ian insists that *Eighteen Inches of Rain* will be his last cowboy culture album, although he allows that he might do one more of older songs if he can find enough material that hasn't been done to death. Right now he feels as though he has said all that he wants to say about breaking horses, droughts, and saddles in the rain. After appearing to coast for a couple of albums and after wrestling with writer's block, the experience of co-writing and working in Nashville brought him out of his dry spell and recaptured much of the freshness of the first three cowboy culture albums. The backing musicians have that indefinable, undeniable Nashville edge—loose but utterly cohesive. Ben Keith, once of the Great Speckled Bird, sat in on steel guitar.

> "Ian's a tough son-of-a-gun. If he says *Eighteen Inches of Rain* will be the last, it will probably be. I sometimes feel like I've given what I have to give and it's time to move on, and I'd certainly understand it if Ian felt the same way. If he gets popular on Vanguard Records, he'll be pressed to stay in the mode, but he's good at keeping to his own agenda. If you're a promoter and you want Ian Tyson, you do things pretty much on his terms."
>
> —*(Hal Cannon, 1994)*

Sixty years is a watershed. The process of looking back and reflecting inevitably leads to thoughts of what might have been. To the oldest unanswerable question, "What if I had it to do over?" Ian, like everyone else, will answer that you have to learn from your own mistakes, not someone else's. No one can go to a manual to figure out what to do next; you have to blunder forward the only way you know how and hope for the best.

"It's taken me twenty-five, thirty years to learn a lot of what I needed to know at the beginning. It hasn't all come easily. Take guitar playing. I'm not one of these guys who pick up a guitar once a week and play circles around everyone else. I have to practice every day with a metronome to play at a good professional level. It's always been that hard. When my second chance came around, I knew my limitations better. I knew I had to practice, and I had learned how to sing and perform. None of those things came naturally to me. I had to painfully learn every one of those.

"I never got a second chance like that in horse breeding. Charlie Araujo, the Californian vaquero breeder who pretty well started Doc Bar's career, said, you don't get a second chance in breeding unless you live to be an old, old man and you have an awful lot of money. You find your stud prospect, probably a yearling, prove him as a performance horse in cutting or roping, and by the time he's proven himself he'll be five. You start breeding him then, and it'll take at least four more years until you find out whether his colts are any good—and that's the proof of the pudding when it comes to breeding horses, and you're already up to about ten years. Then you have to figure out what kind of mares are gonna cross with this horse, and that takes time. You might not find a mare with the right bloodlines to breed with your stud until he's six or seven. It'll be another year before the colt appears, and then it's got to grow up—three or four years. The results might be good, but not sensational . . . and the years go slipping by. Pretty soon, you've got a good breeding horse, but not a world-class horse. Now he's old. For a long time, I said my horse didn't get the excellent mares, but that's not true. He's had some real good mares, and he has produced a few winners, but I would never forgive conformation faults such as he has if I were to do it again. I would never overlook a conformation fault in a prospective breeding sire. Back then, I listened to some wrong advice coming up out of Texas.

"The sire must not have conformation faults to any great degree. He's got to have the good mind, the willingness to perform and the big heart, and that athletic ability. My horse is now over twenty. He has a good mind, a pretty good heart, and he was a terrific athlete, but he had conformation faults."

So, by not starting early enough and not listening to others, Ian hasn't bred another Doc Bar. Even so, there ought to be a measure of contentment to be had in what he has accomplished. He's approaching the age when fall's first chill is usually the cue to load up the Winnebago and head for the sun belt. Instead, Ian has the same restlessness that led him to stand on the highway south of Vancouver, not knowing or caring if he went east or south.

"The big plan on the big horizon isn't there. I'd be all for it if I knew what it was. I've always moved on after ten, twelve, fourteen years . . . and now there's no place to go. It's not that there aren't consolations. I've got the best woman in the world. A wonderful little girl. We're driving new trucks. We could be in Bosnia. But I just feel it's time to try something different.

"A big change came over our lives when Twylla had an accident on July 7, 1992. She got bucked off and broke her back. That accident traumatized us. We didn't know if she would ever walk again. We got a wonderful surgeon who performed a miraculous operation on her

Ian, Twylla, and Adelita at home, 1991. Photograph © by Jay Dusard.

and another one later to remove all the hardware inside her back. He gave her back her life. Before that, our life was ride, ride, ride, and cowboy neighboring with the big ranches west of here. Having Adelita changed that to some extent, and then Twylla's wreck changed it altogether. She still hasn't been back on a horse. I'm sure she'll ride in a recreational way, but I don't think she'll go back to the hard riding.

"I can't ride and train as I used to, and that accident made us realize how fleeting it all can be. There are fewer and fewer places left to go to live the life I want to live. If I go west, I'm in suburban British Columbia. I've been there. Even Nevada's going. It's the final chapter."

For six decades, Ian Tyson has always been able to recognize the next step and has always had the self-confidence to go for it. The self-confidence hasn't deserted him, but sometimes he feels that the options have.

Joan Baez and the Kingston Trio, who played the circuit Ian once played, are out there making the rounds as a double act, inviting forty- and fifty-somethings to remember when. Ian could be out there with them—another Ian & Sylvia comeback tour. Instead, he has beaten off his writer's block, and he's in his line shack, writing perhaps the finest song of his career. It's all there in one song; Jack Kerouac's existential restlessness, the Sons of the Pioneers' cowboy mysticism, and old Roy Acuff's Biblical invocations.

Ian, 1993. Photograph by Ellen Brodylo and Mike Morrow.

Will James

music and lyrics by
IAN TYSON

When I was but a small boy, my fath-er bought me ma-ny books 'bout the crea-tures of the ri-ver banks and the sins of old sea crooks. But the ones I ne-ver left be-hind with the old for-got-ten games, were the tales of wild and win-dy slopes and the man they called Will James. 2. The liv-ing of his cow-boy dreams, or so it seemed to me

the per - fect com - bin - a - tion, rid - ing

high and liv - ing free. His her - oes were his

hor - ses and he drew them clear and true, on ev - ery

page they'd come a - live and jump straight out at

you. **Chorus** And his race to - ward the

sun - set was the high and the lone - some kind. Like the

coy - ote al - ways look - in' back, he left no tracks be -

hind. So I've mem - or - ized those pict - ures, boys, they're

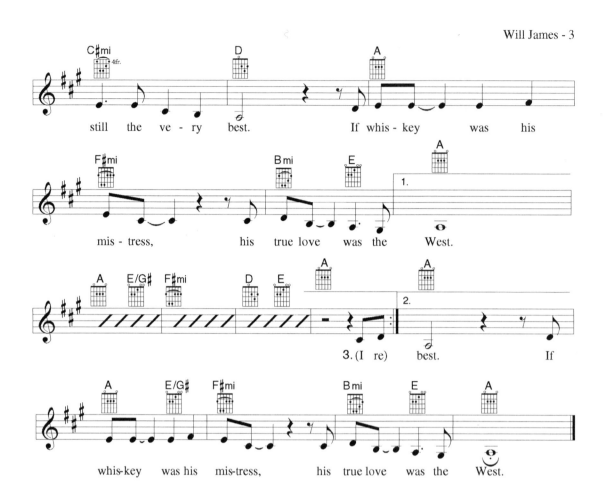

3. I remember up on Dead Man Creek
   back twenty years and more,
   I hired on to breaking colts,
   which I'd never done before.
   A city kid I asked myself,
   "Now what would Will James do?"
   And, you know, it was the damndest thing,
   but it kind of got me through.

Navajo Rug

Music and Lryics by
IAN TYSON
and
TOM RUSSELL

Well, it's two eggs up on whis-key toast, home fries on the side, wash it down with road - house cof-fee, burns up your in - sides. Just a canyon, Co-lo-ra-do din-er and a wait-ress I did love, I sat in the back 'neath an old stuffed bear and a worn-out Na-va-jo rug. Now Old Jack, the boss, he left at six and it's Ka-tie bar the door.

She'd pull down that Na-va-jo rug and she'd spread it 'cross the floor.

Hey I saw light-ning 'cross the sa-cred moun-tains, saw

wo-ven tur-tle doves, I was ly-in' next to Ka-

tie — on that old Na-va-jo rug. Aye, aye,

aye, — Kat-tie — shades of red and

blue. Aye, aye, aye, — Ka-tie — what

ev - er be-came of the Na-va-jo rug and

you? Kat-tie — shades of red and

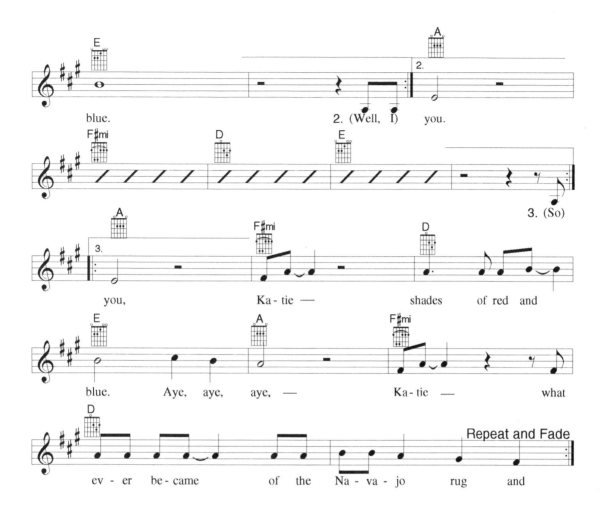

blue.   2. (Well, I) you.

3. (So)

you,   Ka - tie —   shades   of red and

blue.   Aye,   aye,   aye, —   Ka - tie —   what

Repeat and Fade

ev - er be - came   of   the   Na - va - jo   rug   and

2. Well, I saw Old Jack about a year ago,
   he said,"The place burned to the ground.
   And all I saved was this here old bear tooth,
   and Katie she left town.
   But Katie she got her souvenir too,"
   Jack spat a tobacco plug,
   "You should have seen her
   a comin' through the smoke
   dragging that Navajo rug."

3. So every time I cross the sacred mountains
   and lightning breaks above,
   it always takes me back in time
   to my long lost Katie love.
   But everything keeps on a movin'
   and everybody's on the go.
   You don't find things that last anymore
   like an old woven Navajo.

music and lyrics by
IAN TYSON

Fifty Years Ago

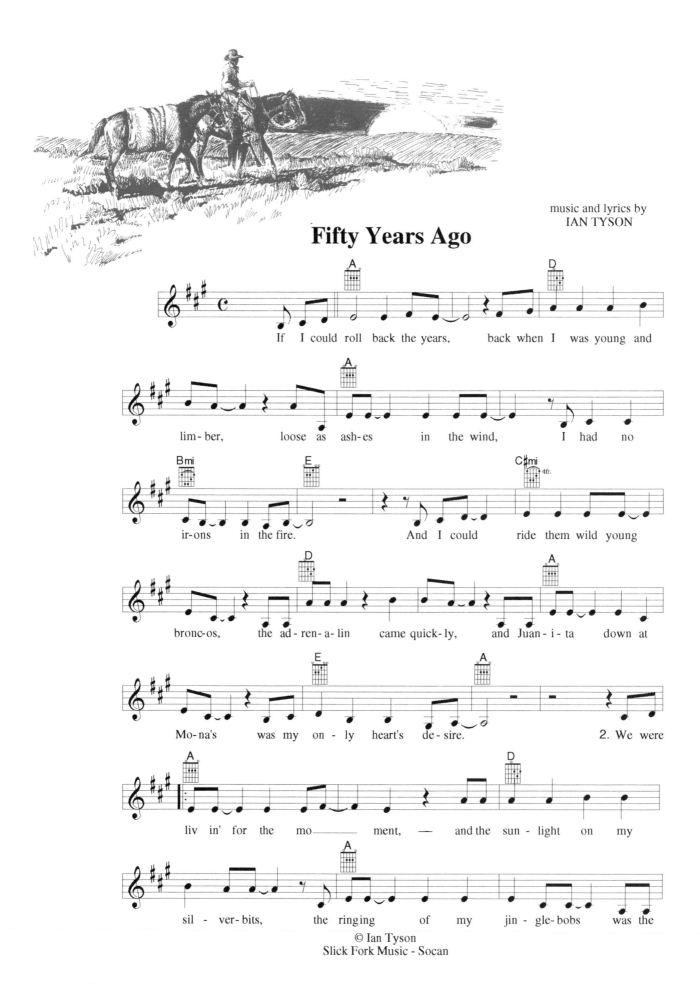

If I could roll back the years, back when I was young and limber, loose as ash-es in the wind, I had no ir-ons in the fire. And I could ride them wild young bronc-os, the ad-ren-a-lin came quick-ly, and Juan-i-ta down at Mo-na's was my on-ly heart's de-sire. 2. We were liv in' for the mo——ment, — and the sun-light on my sil-ver-bits, the ring-ing of my jin-gle-bobs was the

music of my soul. In the al-ley back of Mo-na's I held Juan - i-ta in the shad-ows. How we held on-to each oth-er and the lov-in' that we stole, — Chorus And the sigh-ing of the pines up here near the tim-ber-line makes me wish I'd done things diff-erent. Ah but wish-in' don't make it so. Oh the time has passed so quick, the years all run to-geth-er now. Did I hold Juan - i-ta

To Coda

yes - ter - day? Was it fif - ty years a -

1. E 2. E

D.S. al Coda

go? 3. (If I) go? To Chorus (And the)

go?

Instrumental

Bmi E C#mi

D A

E A

3. If I would have quit them broncos,
   she might have quit that business,
   but that was back in the fast days—
   you know, before the wire.
   I bet I could still find her
   and I bet she's still as pretty
   as when she's Juanita down at Mona's
   and my only heart's desire.

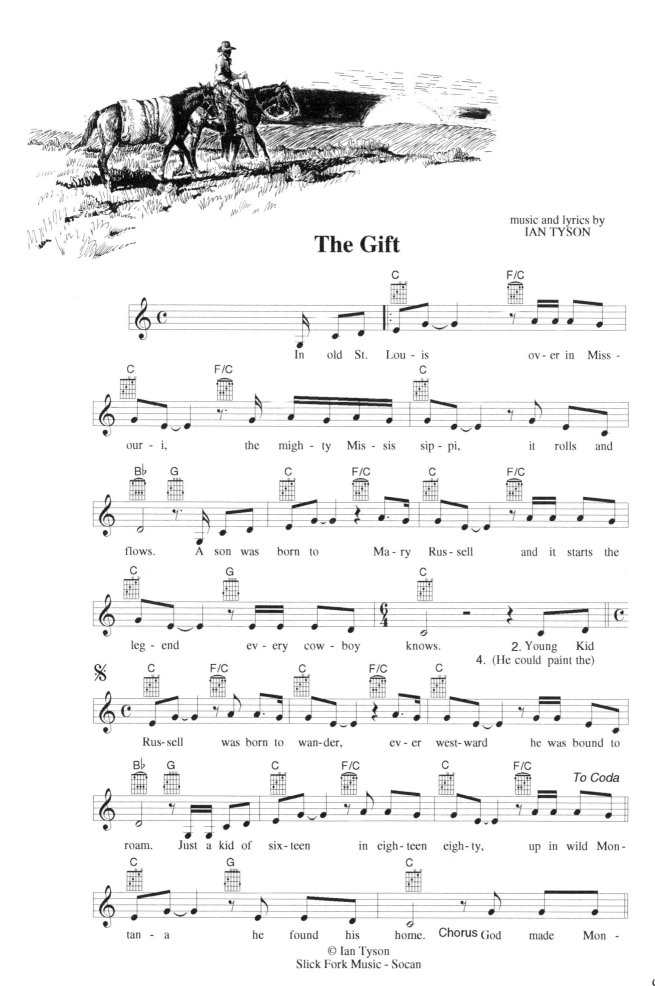

music and lyrics by
IAN TYSON

The Gift

In old St. Lou - is   ov - er in Miss -

our - i,   the migh - ty Mis - sis sip - pi,   it rolls and

flows.   A son was born to   Ma - ry Rus - sell   and it starts the

leg - end   ev - ery cow - boy   knows.   2. Young   Kid
4. (He could paint the)

Rus - sell   was born to wan - der,   ev - er west - ward   he was bound to

To Coda

roam.   Just a kid of six - teen   in eigh - teen eigh - ty,   up in wild Mon -

tan - a   he found his   home. **Chorus** God   made Mon -

© Ian Tyson
Slick Fork Music - Socan

tan-a for the wild man, for the Pei-gan, and the Sioux and Crow, but He saved His

great-est gift for Char-lie, said, "Get her all down be-fore she

goes, — you 'got-ta get her all down 'cause she's bound to go."

1.

2.

D.S. al Coda

3.(God hung the)

5.(When the Lord called)

paint them quite as good as you. And when you're done go out and have a

few, and Nan-cy Rus-sell will make sure it's just two. God made Mon-

tan-a for the wild man, for the Pei gan, and the Sioux and Crow, but He saved His

great-est   gift for Char - lie,   said, "Get her all down   be - fore   she

goes, —   you 'got-ta get her all down 'cause she's bound to go."   Said, "Get her all

3. God hung the stars over Judith Basin.
   God put the magic in young Charlie's hand.
   All was seen and all remembered —
   every shining mountain, every longhorn brand.

4. He could paint the light on the horsehide shining,
   great passing heards of the buffalo,
   and a cow camp cold on a rainy morning,
   and the twisting wrist of the Houlihan throw.

   Repeat Chorus

5. When the Lord called Charlie to His home up yonder,
   he said, "Kid Russell, I got a job for you.
   You're in charge of sunsets in old Montana
   'cause I can't paint them quite as good as you.
   And when you're done — go out and have a few,
   and Nancy Russell will make sure it's just two."

   Repeat Chorus

Someday Soon

music and lyrics by
IAN TYSON

There's a young man that I know, his age is twen-ty one,
he comes from down in south-ern Col-or-a-do,
Just out of the ser-vice, and he's look-in' for his fun. Some-day
soon, I'm going with him, some-day soon. 2. My
par-ents can-not stand him 'cause he works the ro-de-o.
My dad-dy says that he will leave me cry-ing, but
I will fol-low him right down the tough-est row to hoe, some-day
soon, go-ing with him some-day soon.

When he comes to call my Pa ain't got a good word to say, 'cause he was just as wild in his young-er days. 3. So blow you old blue north-er, blow him back to me. He's driv-in' in to-night from Cal-i-for_____nia. He loves those damned old ro-de-os as much as he loves me. Some-day soon, I'm going with him some-day soon. soon. Some-day soon, I'm going with him some-day soon.

97

Jaquima To Freno

music and lyrics by
IAN TYSON
and
B. McINTYRE

Ja-qui-ma to Fren-o — he's an old va-quer-o from an-oth-er time, hands as fine as the deal-ers of Re-no. He's been to the o-cean, he's been to the sea. Big long tap-a-der-os hang-in' both sides of an old vis-a-li-a tree. Hey, mis-ter va-quer-o, put a han-dle on my po-ny for me, teach me the mys-ter-y. y. Did they sing all day? Did they dance all night? Did they

ride their spade bit po-nies through the gol-den light? Did they
find true love? Was it all a bunch of lies?
spoken___ Quim Sa be, may-be it was par-a-dise.___
To Coda
Instrumental
rit.

2. Jaquima to Freno —
    he's an old amansador,
    still hangin' on, almost gone,
    like the California condor.
    He's been down to the rodear ground,
    seen him on the movie screen,
    sometimes I think he's like America —
    only see him in my dreams.
    Hey, mister vaquero,
    put a handle on my pony for me,
    teach me the mystery.

3. Jaquima to Freno —
    he's an old vaquero
    from another time, hands as fine
    as the dealers of Reno.
    He's been to the ocean,
    he's been to the sea
    Big long tapaderos hangin' both sides
    of an old visalia tree.
    Hey, mister vaquero,
    put a handle on my pony for me,
    teach me the mystery.

Magpie

music and lyrics by
IAN TYSON

Mag - pie, you're an ear - ly ris - er. Mag - pie, you're a bold chas - tis - er. Mag - pie — al - ways wak - ing up my wife and I, you old coy - o - te in the sky. Mag - pie, some say, you're a bold de - ceiv - er, I say, you're a true be - liev - er. Mag - pie — ah, the West ain't ne - ver gon - na die — just as long as you can fly. You

Bridge

roam all ar - ound these hills like a gyp - sy, I don't see what's the mat - ter with that. You're choice is meat for some - thing to eat — I don't have a prob - lem with that. You build a big house with a front and a back door, and you want to be free.

2nd Bridge. You hang all around these hills
in the wintertime—
why in the hell would you want to do that?
If it was me I'd be out of here man—
Give me a couple seconds and I'll grab my hat.
Ah, magpie, you're a pretty bird,
you just want to be free—
Holy Moses magpie,
I am you, you are me.

music and lyrics by
IAN TYSON

M.C. Horses

We were hav-ing a drink at Stock - men's, list-ening to the gui - tars ring, Jes - se said, "You know they sold the M. C. hor - ses."

(spoken) "I'll be damned, when was that?" — I had - n't heard a thing, "Back in Aug-ust, one hun-dred head and more."

2. Yeah the
4. (If you) peo-ple they come from ev-ery-where just to bid on them high and low, and there-by own a piece of the leg - end.

With the cow herd all dis-persed the old cav-vy she had to go, back in Aug-ust, one hun-dred head and more. *Chorus* So come on boys run 'em in. We're gon-na let this sale be-gin, last of the big rem-u-das of the migh-ty M. C. There's hor-ses here for ev-ery-one, sad-dle 'em kids, let's get her done. By the time that O-re-gon sun goes down this out-fit's his-tor-y.

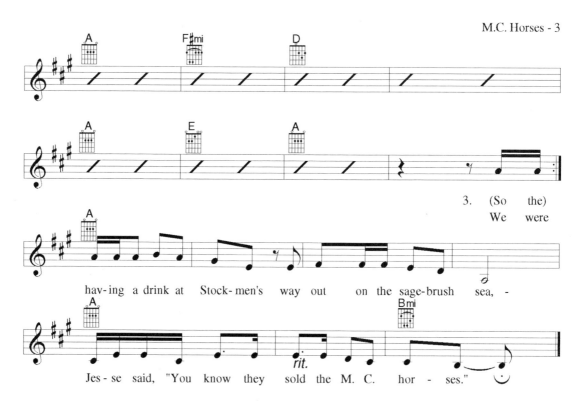

3. (So the)
We were

hav-ing a drink at Stock-men's way out on the sage-brush sea, -

Jes-se said, "You know they sold the M. C. hor - ses."

rit.

3. So the M.C. crew they rode 'em all,
people all gathered 'round.
One 'ol boy gave two grand for Banjo.
Banjo took his trailer apart
when they tried to load him up for town,
back in August, one hundred head and more.

4. If you ever have a beer at the Adel store
say hi to Chuck and Annie,
they'll show you those big 'ol steer heads
up there hangin'.
When you ask where have they gone,
hell they've gone like the M.C. cavvy,
back in August, one hundred head and more.

music and lyrics by
IAN TYSON

Four Strong Winds

Four strong winds that blow lone - ly, sev - en seas that run high. All those things that don't change come what may._____ Our good times have all gone, I'm bound for mov-in' on. I'll look for you if I'm ev-er back this way._____ *Fine* Think I'll 2. (If I) go out to Al - ber - ta, wea-ther's good there in the fall. Got some friends that I can go to work-in'

for. Still I wish you'd change your mind, if I

asked you one more time. But we've been through this a

D.S. al Fine

hun - dred times or more._____ Four strong

2. If I get there before the snow flies,
   if things are looking good,
   I could meet you if I send you down the fare.
   But by then it will be winter,
   not too much for you to do.
   And those winds sure blow cold way out there.

'Til The Circle Is Through

music and lyrics by
IAN TYSON

nights be crowned with a man-tle of stars. May your
po-ny stay sound for the work to be done. He'll get you
home with your dreams and your scars.

3rd Chorus May you stay where the riv-er runs through the
range and the sky,___ buck-skin and blue. May you
ride to the end on the wings___ of the wind 'til you're
home and your cir-cle___ is through.___

2. May the children read, may they understand
   what is of true value, that the truth may be known —
   the glory of God and the dark side of man —
   one day they must ride on alone.

Summer Wages

music and lyrics by
IAN TYSON

Nev-er hit sev-en-teen when you play a-gainst the dealer, for you know —— the odds won't ride with you.

Nev-er leave your wo-man a-lone when your friends are out to steal her, she'll be gam-bled and gone like sum-mer wa——ges.

2. (And we'll)

Bridge In all the beer par-lours all down a-long Main Street, the dreams of the sea-son are all spilled down on the floor. And the big stands of tim-ber —— wait-ing there just for fall-in'. The

hook-ers stand-ing watch-ful-ly, wait-ing by the door. 3. So I'll

work on the tow-boats with my slip-per-y ci-ty shoes on, Lord I

swore I would nev-er do that a-gain —— Through the

great fog-bound straights where the ced-ars stand a-

wait-ing, I'll be far off and gone like sum-mer

wa——ges. To Bridge (In) Years are

gam-bled and lost like sum-mer wa——ges.

2. And we'll keep rollin' on
   'til we get to Vancouver
   and the woman that I love
   who's living there.
   It's been six long months
   and more since I've seen her,
   maybe gambled and gone
   like summer wages.

Discography

Note: Anthologies containing performances by Ian Tyson or Ian & Sylvia have not been included, unless those performances are unavailable elsewhere.

IAN AND SYLVIA

(M) = mono; (S) = stereo.

Ian and Sylvia (Vanguard VRS 9109 (M)/VSD 2113 (S)) 1961 Rocks And Gravel; Old Blue; C.C. Rider; Un Canadien Errant; Handsome Molly; Mary Anne; Pride Of Petrovar; Makes A Long-Time Man Feel Bad; Rambler Gambler; Got No More Home Than A Dog; When First Unto This Country; Live a-Humble; Down By The Willow Garden

Four Strong Winds (Vanguard VRS 9133 (M)/VSD 2149 (S)) 1963 Jesus Met The Woman At The Well; Tomorrow Is A Long Time; Katy Dear; Poor Lazarus; Four Strong Winds; Ella Speed; Long Lonesome Road; V'la l'Bon Vent; Royal Canal; Lady Of Carlisle; Spanish Is A Loving Tongue; The Greenwood Sidie; Every Night When The Sun Goes Down; Every Time I Feel The Spirit

Evening Concerts At Newport, Vol. 1 (Vanguard VRS 9148 (M)/VSD 79148 (S)) 1963 Un Canadien Errant (balance of album by other artists)

Northern Journey (Vanguard VRS 9154 (M)/VSD 79154 (S)) 1964 You Were On My Mind; Moonshine Can; The Jealous Lover; Four Rode By; Brave Wolfe; Nova Scotia Farewell; Some Day Soon; Little Beggarman; Texas Rangers; The Ghost Lovers; Captain Woodstock's Courtship; Green Valley; Swing Down Chariot

Early Morning Rain (Vanguard VRS 9175 (M)/VSD 79175 (S)) 1965 Come In Stranger; Early Morning Rain; Nancy Whiskey; Awake Ye Drowsy Sleepers; Marlborough Street Blues; Darcy Farrow; Traveling Drummer; Maude's Blues; Red Velvet; I'll Bid My Heart Be Still; For Lovin' Me; Song For Canada

Play One More (Vanguard VRS 9215 (M)/VSD 79215 (S)) 1966 Short Grass; The French Girl; When I Was A Cowboy; Changes; Gifts Are For Giving; Molly And Tenbrooks; Hey, What About Me?; Lonely Girls; Satisfied Mind; Twenty-Four Hours From Tulsa; Friends Of Mine; Play One More

So Much For Dreaming (Vanguard VRS 9241 (M)/VSD 79241 (S)) 1967 Circle Game; So Much For Dreaming; Wild Geese; Child Apart; Summer Wages; Hold Tight; Cutty Wren; Si Les Bateaux; Catfish Blues; Come All Ye Fair And Tender Ladies; January Morning; Grey Morning

The Best Of (Vanguard VSD 79269) 1968 Compilation from LPs above.

Nashville (Vanguard VRS 9284 (M)/VSD 79284 (S)) 1968 The Mighty Quinn; This Wheel's On Fire; Farewell To The North; Taking Care of Business; Southern Comfort; Ballad Of The Ugly Man; 90 x 90; She'll Be Gone; London Life; The Renegade; House Of Cards

Ian and Sylvia's Greatest Hits, Vol. 1 (Vanguard VSD 3/4) 1969 Compilation from LPs above.

Lovin' Sound (MGM E 4388 (M)/SE 4388 (S)) 1966 Windy Weather; Hang On To A Dream; I Don't Believe You; Where Did All The Love Go?; Mr. Spoons; National Hotel; Sunday; Pilgrimage To Paradise; (Find A) Reason To Believe; Big River; Trilogy; Lovin' Sound

Full Circle (MGM SE 4550) 1968 Here's To You; I Learned From Leah; Woman's World; Mr. Spoons; Shinbone Alley; Please Think; Stories He'd Tell; Jinkson Johnson; Tears Of Rage; The Minstrel

GREAT SPECKLED BIRD

Great Speckled Bird (Ampex A 10103) 1969 Love What You're Doing Child; Calgary; Trucker's Cafe; Long Long Time To Get Old; Flies In The Bottle; Bloodshot Beholder; Crazy Arms; This Dream; Smiling Wine; Rio Grande; Disappearing Woman; We Sail

IAN & SYLVIA AND GREAT SPECKLED BIRD

Ian & Sylvia (Columbia C 30736) 1971 More Often Than Not; Creators Of Rain; Summer Wages; Midnight; Barney; Some Kind Of Fool; Shark And The Cockroach; Last Lonely Eagle; Lincoln Freed Me; Needle Of Death; Everybody Has To Say Goodbye

You Were On My Mind (Columbia KC 31337) 1972 Get Up Jake; Old Cheyenne; Antelope; Miriam; Lonesome Valley; You Were On My Mind; Joshua; You're Not Alone Any More; Salmon In The Sea; The Beginning Of The End; Bill (Won't You Please Take Me Home)

The Best of Ian & Sylvia (Columbia G-32516) 1973 (Contains C-30736 and KC-31337).

IAN TYSON

Ol Eon (A&M SP 9017) 1974 Some Kind Of Fool; Bad Times Were So Easy; Blueberry Susan; Sam Bonnifield's Saloon; If She Just Helps Me; Lord, Lead Me Home; Great Canadian Tour; She's My Greatest Blessing; Spanish Johnny; The Girl Who Turned Me Down; The North Saskatchewan; Love Can Bless The Soul Of Anyone

One Jump Ahead of the Devil (Boot BOS 7189) 1978 What Does She See?; One Jump Ahead Of The Devil; Beverly; Turning Thirty; Newtonville Waltz; Lone Star And Coors; One Too Many; Texas, I Miss You; Goodness of Shirley; Freddie Hall; Half Mile Of Hell (Note: Reissued on CD as Stony Plain SPCD 1177; cassette SP5-1177)

Old Corrals and Sagebrush (Columbia PCC 80080) 1983 Gallo De Cielo; Alberta's Child; The Old Double Diamond; Windy Bill; Montana Waltz; Whoopee Ti-Yi-Yo; Leavin' Cheyenne; Old Corrals And Sagebrush; Old Alberta Moon; Diamond Joe; Night Rider's Lament (Note: Reissued on cassette as Stony Plain SP5-1106)

The Interview (Columbia CDN 123) 1983 Interview disc. Issued for promotion only.

Ian Tyson (Columbia FC 39362) 1984 Oklahoma Hills; Tom Blasingame; Sierra Peaks; Colorado Trail; Hot Summer Tears; What Does She See; Rocks Begin To Roll; Will James; Brazos; Murder Steer; Goodnight Loving Trail (Note: Reissued on cassette as Stony Plain SP5-1114)

Cowboyography (Eastern Slope LP ESL 01; Stony Plain LP SPL 1102; cassette SP5-1102) 1986 Springtime; Navajo Rug; Summer Wages; Fifty Years Ago; Rockies Turn Rose; Claude Dallas; Own Heart's Delight; The Gift; Cowboy Pride; Old Cheyenne; The Coyote And The Cowboy (Note: Reissued on CD as Stony Plain SPCD 1102)

Old Corrals and Sagebrush & Other Cowboy Culture Classics (Bear Family/Stony Plain CD BCD 15437) 1988 Gallo De Cielo; Alberta's Child; The Old Double Diamond; Windy Bill; Montana Waltz; Whoopee Ti-Yi-Yo; Leavin' Cheyenne; Old Corrals And Sagebrush; Old Alberta Moon; Night Rider's Lament; Oklahoma Hills; Tom Blasingame; Colorado Trail; Hot Summer Tears; What Does She See; Rocks Begin To Roll; Will James; Murder Steer.

Frutigen Switzerland 1987 Live (Kander Records, Switzerland, LP140188) 1987 Live recordings with Andrew Hardin: Summer Wages; Someday Soon.

I Outgrew the Wagon (Stony Plain LP SPL 1131; CD SPCD 1131; cassette SP5-1131) 1989 Cowboys Don't Cry; Casey Tibbs; I Outgrew The Wagon; Arms Of Corey Jo; Adelita Rose; Irving Berlin Is 100 Years Old Today; Since The Rain; The Wind In The Wire; Four Strong Winds; The Banks Of The Musselshell; The Steeldust Line

And Stood There Amazed (Stony Plain CD SPCD 1168; cassette SP5-1168) 1991 Black Nights; Lights Of Laramie; Jaquima To Freno; Springtime In Alberta; Non-Pro Song; Milk River Ridge; Rocks Begin To Roll; Jack Link; You're Not Alone; Magpie; Home On The Range

Promotional CD (Warner Music Canada CD PRO 91095) 1991 Ian Tyson radio ID and interview.

Ian Tyson (Stony Plain promotional cassette SP5-PRO 1) 1992 Lights of Laramie; Magpie; I Outgrew the Wagon; Navajo Rug (Cassette issued for promotion only)

Tom Russell: Cowboy Real (Stony Plain CD SPCD 1176; cassette SP5-1176/Philo CD 1146) 1992 Two duets with Ian Tyson: Navajo Rug; Gallo del Cielo.

Eighteen Inches of Rain (Stony Plain CD SPCD 1193; cassette SP5-1193/Vanguard CD 79475) 1994 Horsethief Moon; Heartaches Are Stealin'; Eighteen Inches Of Rain; M.C. Horses; Big Horns; Old House; Chasin' The Moon; Nobody Thought It Would; Rodeo Road; Alcohol In The Bloodstream; Old Corrals And Sagebrush; 'Til The Circle Is Through

Ian Tyson (Stony Plain promotion CD PRO-IAN 94) 1994 Horsethief Moon; Heartaches Are Stealin'; Rodeo Road; Alcohol In The Bloodstream; Since The Rain; I Outgrew The Wagon; You're Not Alone; Navajo Rug; Ian Tyson speaks with Jim Rooney, co-producer of "Eighteen Inches Of Rain."

Note: All commercial Stony Plain releases are available from Stony Plain Records, P.O. Box 861, Edmonton, Alberta, Canada T5J 2L8.

With thanks to Holger Petersen, Richard Flohil, and Richard Weize.